IN RELENTLESS PURSUIT OF ME

Upending the Unicorn Effect

AN AUTOETHNOGRAPHIC EXPLORATION
BY BLACK WOMEN

Copyright © 2025 Hunter Street Press

ISBN Hardcover: 978-1-967071-98-2

ISBN eBook: 978-1-967071-99-9

Book design by: TeaBerryStudio.com

ENDORSEMENTS FOR
In Relentless Pursuit of Me

I felt empowered and validated. Like I belonged to a sorority rooted not in school, but in shared ancestry. As a Black woman, I've carried burdens I didn't choose—unfair expectations, isolation, and silence. These women's stories made me feel seen, heard, and no longer alone.

Reading this book felt like sitting in a sacred circle of sisters—raw, real, and restorative. It speaks to the strength we carry and the stories we've long needed to share.

—DARNNELL REESE

What a beautiful curation of Black women storytellers! "In Relentless Pursuit: Upending the Unicorn Effect" reveals those added layers in our varied experiences as Black women. This book is timely on so many levels. It comes when OUR stories are being dismantled and dismissed from public platforms. Thank you for telling, writing, and preserving these narratives for US!

—PAULETTE HARRIS-GROSS

Women are truly magical—far braver than we often give ourselves credit for. When we find the courage to use our voices, to be vulnerable and share our stories, we create space for connection, healing, and community. The words of these authors made me laugh, brought me to tears, and inspired deep reflection on my own journey.

These powerful and authentic stories made me laugh, cry, and reflect—while reminding me of the strength found in vulnerability and connection.

In Relentless Pursuit is a powerful testament to the strength, resilience, and brilliance of Black women. As a white woman, I was deeply moved by the honesty and authenticity of each story. These women pushed through unimaginable challenges—not because it was easy, but because giving up was never an option. Their strength often came from necessity, and their perseverance is both humbling and inspiring. The words written by these authors is a reminder of the magic that happens when women find a support system and realize they are not alone. It's a celebration of courage, community, resilience, and authenticity.

—JACQUELINE CETERA

The Relentless Pursuit of Upending the Unicorn Effect is a must have and read for EVERY Black woman! I smiled, I cried and I cheered as I read this wonderful book from these wise women. The auto ethnographies are not just stories of relatable lived experiences, but every entry is a masterclass on recognizing how the Unicorn Effect shows up and how to thrive…even in spaces designed for our demise. This will be a book that you will read and re-read at various turns of your workplace and life's journey!

—NIA K. DAVIS

Reading the stories shared by the book's contributors, I found echoes of my own experiences, struggles, and dreams woven into their journeys. Recognizing familiar traits in their resilience, growth, and self-discovery made me feel seen and understood. It reminded me that I'm not alone on my path and gave me the clarity and courage to make choices that align more closely with who I'm meant to be.

—NIA F. MASON, PHD

This is a good read for young women in their formative years to inspire them and help them to understand that obstacles may come, but they are surmountable.

—GINA MALDONADO DUPART

Brilliantly written! In *Relentless Pursuit of Me* truly captures the full essence of what it means to embody Black Girl Magic in the face of adversity. This beautiful work will share a sacred space on my bookshelf next to my copy of "For Colored Girls," for they are one and the same!

—MARI WILLIAMS

Relentless Pursuit of Me is a collection of powerful storytelling and shared experience not often found in other works of this type. This is an incredibly strong group of women with abundant life lessons. The reader is a witness to the pain and challenges surmounted in the workplace and in society. As a white male it was uncomfortable to hear what these women experience in the workplace, which is the point. We can only learn and change when we see and attempt to understand other's lived realities.

—GEORGE FISCUS

These women go a long way to define their thoughts and goals. A must-read for all seeking to understand Black women in the workplace.

—DICK MUELLER

IN RELENTLESS PURSUIT OF ME

UPENDING THE UNICORN EFFECT

RONICKA BRISCOE, PH.D.

BOOK DEDICATION

*I am reminded of your sincere faith,
which first lived in your grandmother…*

2 TIMOTHY 1:5 NIV

In Relentless Pursuit of Me could not have come to be without the women who came before us.

This work is a love letter to our grandmothers; to their courage, their sacrifice, and their unwavering faith. So many of their stories were never written down—only whispered in kitchens, passed down in lullabies, or carried through oral histories between generations. To our grandmothers who dared to dream in silence, who pushed forward even when the world told them to sit still, who loved deeply, led quietly, and lived courageously. We walk in the power of their legacy, standing tall on the foundation they laid.

We are the answers to the prayers they prayed, the fruit of their labor, the dreams they never had the chance to dream out loud. It is because of *them* that we have the strength to pursue every part of who we are—fully, boldly, relentlessly.

Honor their journeys.
Live in their light.

Say their names:

Paula Butler
Iceola Ellzey
Joyce Bush Harrison
Elizabeth Luster
Ida Mae Wilkes Olds
Agnes Marie Jones Ormond
Mattie Palmer
Rose Carter Pierre
Bertha Reese
Mary Roussell
Ella Mae Savoy
Charlotte Simon
Bernice McCormick White
Othella Williams

CONTENTS

Foreword xv
Introduction xix

Introduction to Ronicka Briscoe 1
In Relentless Pursuit of...
Upending the Unicorn Effect 5

Introduction to Monica Pierre 11
In Relentless Pursuit of... My Voice 13

Introduction to Dorothy Doolittle 25
In Relentless Pursuit of... Enoughness 29

Introduction to Aaron Harrison 55
In Relentless Pursuit of... Autonomy 57

Introduction to Dominique Luster 77
In Relentless Pursuit of... Legacy 79

Introduction to Ebony Allen 95
In Relentless Pursuit of... Peace 97

Introduction to Jawan Brown Alexander 115
In Relentless Pursuit of... Purpose 117

Introduction to Chanise Reese-Queen 135
In Relentless Pursuit of... Infinite Potential 137

Introduction to LaShon Ormond 159
In Relentless Pursuit of... Sisterhood 161

Epilogue 181
Acknowledgements 185
Discussion Guide Questions 189

FOREWORD

BY
MONICA PIERRE

Stories have power. This truth has anchored my work for nearly forty years as a reporter, producer and talk show host, and continues as the foundation of my work as a university professor. I've witnessed firsthand how authentic narratives can challenge assumptions, connect divided communities, and catalyze transformation.

The most compelling stories contain an undeniable truth that, once spoken, cannot be unheard. They don't merely document; they shine light. They don't simply inform; they transform. This is why, in my Emmy award-winning career, I've relentlessly pursued stories that matter—especially those coming from marginalized communities and the voiceless.

For Black women, storytelling has always been an act of courage. Our narratives are frequently filtered, diminished, or erased altogether. Our complex truths compressed into stereotypes. Our wisdom mischaracterized, our directness misinterpreted, our strength misconstrued.

In an era where authentic histories face erasure, these eight autoethnographic accounts arrive with urgency and importance. Each contributor has demonstrated what can only be described as "bold truth-telling"—connecting personal and professional experiences to broader societal patterns with unflinching honesty. They have refused the convenient and often-time expected path of silence and rejected the temptation to soften their experiences for palatable consumption.

What you hold is not merely a collection of reflections, but resistance documented. It is legacy preserved. As you engage with these pages, I invite you to recognize not only the strength and wisdom contained within but also the transformative potential of your own story. For when we understand the power of authentic storytelling, we recognize that liberation begins with giving voice to what we have long held silent.

The story continues.

INTRODUCTION

SUPER*MAN*
HAS ALWAYS BEEN...

SUPERMAN HAS ALWAYS BEEN A BLACK WOMAN. Yes! You read the sentence correctly, I repeat, Superman has always been a Black woman. Although your American history books may tell you a different story, in every instance the country found itself in crisis, Black women have led social justice movements throughout this history, even when you did not see them. Examples can be found in the Suffrage Movement, Civil Rights Movement, Black Lives Matter Movement, MeToo Movement, and the Modern-Day Civil Rights Movement.

Recently, we saw former President Joe Biden enter the 2024 presidential race that he should have never entered as an aging 80+-year-old White man. America watched as his body seemingly began to deteriorate right before our eyes as he struggled to stand upright. We watched as he got lost in speeches, he slurred his speech and could barely recall important information during interviews—all while a much younger, poised, intelligent woman supported him as Vice President. And with just ninety days before the election, the Democratic party decided to put the cape on Kamala Harris as a last-ditch effort to save the country.

Nationally, Black women account for only 1.6% of vice president roles and a mere 1.4% of chief-level positions (LeanIn.org, 2020). As I write this book, there are only two Black women at the helm of Fortune 500 companies. In 2020, the under-representation of Black women in executive leadership roles inspired me to explore the lived experiences of top-level Black women leaders, the strategies they used to obtain their roles, and the approaches they utilize to navigate their careers and overcome challenges. I explored these questions during my doctoral research in which I interviewed Black Women leaders across the sectors of health care, business, education, and the public sector.

During my research, I discovered largely that Black women were sought out and recruited to their roles because they spent their formative years developing a strong reputation by working hard and making sacrifices. Although the women were recruited to their roles, each still found herself working hard to prove she belonged in her respective position, creating an earned, not-given mentality. So, instead of getting the superstar treatment a highly sought-after candidate would expect, they were marginalized and treated poorly. Additionally, the women believed in doing excellent work, but each was unwilling to sacrifice herself, using each day as a *Relentless Pursuit of Self*.

Although the interviews of the women revealed that Black women in executive leadership roles have multifaceted experiences, these women still prioritized making a bigger impact and bringing others along as they ascended. The women committed to engaging in meaningful work that would positively impact their communities or sectors while also ensuring they are mentoring and positioning others, particularly other Black women, to secure leadership positions.

While in search of these tactical strategies, I listened to the phenomenal Black women recall their professional and personal life experiences; there was an undeniable phenomenon that every woman was experiencing, unbeknownst to them.

While society has often searched for Superman, a heroic figure who can come in and save the day, there is now a search for something even more elusive: the "Unicorn." The term *unicorn* has come to represent the impossible expectations placed on individuals—those expected to juggle a mix of unrelated, misaligned job responsibilities, take on the workload of three people while being paid less than one, and single-handedly rescue organizations that have been operating in dysfunction for years, if not decades. In professional job posts as well as casual conversations, you hear the call, "We need a unicorn." Oftentimes, this search for a unicorn ends with a Black woman because she is most educated, has the experience, and can do the job, but the unrealistic, often unattainable expectations and lack of resources makes the work nearly impossible, yet she often takes on the challenge anyway.

During my research, I found that the intersectional identities of Black women create multifaceted experiences that transpire simultaneously in their lives: ***internally and externally; personally, and professionally; and in the past, present, and future.*** Kimberlé Crenshaw, who is well known because she first coined the term intersectionality, is quoted as saying "There was no name for this problem. And we all know that where there's no name for a problem, you can't see a problem, and when you can't see a problem, you pretty much can't solve it." Because there was no name for this experience, I named it the "**Unicorn Effect**."

The unicorn is often depicted as a mythical creature that can do any and all things, similar to the popularized term of endearment, *Black girl magic*. Others, such as Simone Biles, embrace the title of the GOAT, the *greatest of all times*; however, the *Unicorn Effect* encompasses the added pressure Black women experience when attempting to maintain a strong sense of self-identity while over-performing for no recognition and sacrificing personal goals while also focusing on the holistic impact of their work and making space for others to succeed.

This level of expectation is unrealistic, taxing, and unmanageable for any human. Black women navigate these multifaceted layers, get their work done, and appear inhuman, mythical, like a unicorn.

Vice President Kamala Harris lived out the Unicorn Effect for the entire world to see. After Joe Biden was forced to relinquish the Democratic nomination for presidency, Vice President Harris was offered the nomination. Not because it should have been hers in the first place, but because the party was fearful. She had the impossible task of uniting a divided democratic party, trying to convince the American people that she could do the job despite her impeccable resume and education, and not to mention convincing the people that she could do a better job than a convicted felon. She had ninety days to convince voters that they were ready for a Black Woman president. Despite her best efforts, she faced significant challenges, many of which directly related to her intersectional identities, including racial identity as being Black and Asian, being a woman, not having biological children, and other factors. Both her personal and professional lives were interrogated and dissected.

THE UNICORN EFFECT EXPLAINED

The Unicorn Effect can be formally defined as *a phenomenon in which Black women are expected to perform under intense and often unrealistic demands in both professional and personal realms, embodying resilience and adaptability to "make something out of nothing" and "do more with less." Characterized by high expectations to excel despite systemic obstacles, the Unicorn Effect reflects the pressures Black women face to hold families and organizations together, navigate isolation in the workplace, manage behind-the-scenes responsibilities without recognition, juggle multiple roles, and endure pay inequities—all while still achieving excellence and success.*

Internal refers to the private and introspective dimensions of Black women's lives, encompassing their thoughts, emotions, and self-perception. These internal experiences may involve navigating imposter syndrome, self-doubt, or self-empowerment as they reconcile their unique identities with societal expectations of them.

External relates to the outward-facing aspects of their identities, including how they are perceived, judged, or treated by others. This includes interactions within professional environments, societal stereotypes, and external pressures to conform to traditional norms or cultural expectations.

Personal encompasses the non-work-related areas of their lives, such as family, friendships, romantic relationships, community engagement, and culture. Personal experiences within the Unicorn Effect highlight the challenges of balancing familial obligations, maintaining cultural authenticity, and preserving personal well-being while advancing professionally.

Professional refers to the roles, responsibilities, and expectations Black women navigate within their careers. It includes their interactions with colleagues, leadership decisions, career advancement, and professional reputation. This term also encompasses the challenges they face in breaking through systemic barriers, addressing workplace biases, and excelling in environments where they may be one of the few—or the only—women of color in leadership positions.

Professionally, they often find themselves balancing the need to deliver exceptional results while advocating for diversity, equity, and inclusion, all while challenging traditional leadership norms and stereotypes. This aspect of the Unicorn Effect highlights how their multifaceted identities uniquely influence their professional impact and contributions.

Past represents the historical and ancestral influences that shape the lived experiences of Black women. This includes the legacy of systemic oppression, the achievements of trailblazing Black women, and personal life experiences that have contributed to their resilience.

Present refers to the current realities and daily experiences of Black women as they navigate their multifaceted identities in today's world. It captures their ongoing efforts to balance intersectional challenges, such as responding to workplace dynamics, asserting their presence in underrepresented or undervalued spaces, and managing societal and cultural expectations. For some, this may include navigating the pressures of the biological clock if they have not yet married or had children, while others may be balancing the demands of family life, marriage, and caring for aging parents. These present realities reflect the complex interplay of personal and professional responsibilities that shape their leadership journeys and lived experiences.

Future symbolizes their aspirations, goals, and vision for what they hope to achieve both personally and professionally. This includes their desire to pave the way for future generations of Black women leaders and to redefine the leadership paradigms through their lived experiences and innovative approaches.

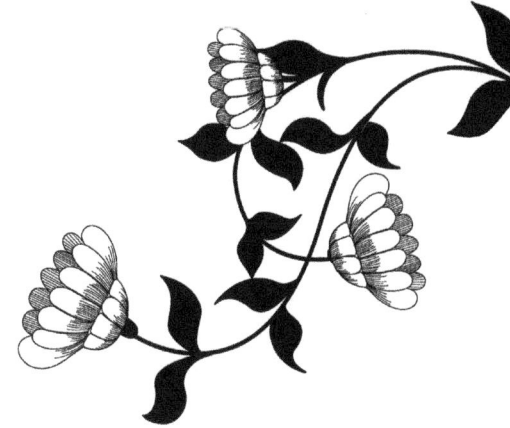

Introduction to
RONICKA BRISCOE

Dr. Ronicka Briscoe, nationally recognized educator, scholar, and leader brings her talent and nearly twenty years of professional experience to her new role as Founder and CEO of Winning on the Road, LLC, the premier organization for Elevating Leaders and Igniting Team Transformation through professional learning, executive coaching, and customized leadership development programs.

Dr. Briscoe serves as Principal researcher, lead consultant and expert facilitator where she brings a unique speaking and presentation style in which she seamlessly weaves together her extensive research, rich lived experiences, and expertise. This combination creates a dynamic and impactful experience that captivates her audience from start to finish and propels them to act.

Dr. Ronicka Briscoe is a highly esteemed leader recognized for her significant contributions and impactful work. Her accolades include being named among the Women We Admire Top CEOs—2025, Women We Admire—Top Women Leaders for 2024 and New Orleans Magazine's

Women of Impact in 2024. Her impressive list of honors also includes being a recipient of the 2023 Xavier University of Louisiana 40 under 40 award, the 2022 and 2024 New Orleans City Business Woman of the Year, the 2023 Teach for America Community Leader of the Year, and the 2022 University of Holy Cross Community Service Award.

Ronicka is an interdisciplinary scholar and practitioner whose career and community work spans nearly two decades. Ronicka formally studied political science, public administration (non-profit management), business, and executive leadership. She has spent her career in education as a teacher, administrator, professor, university department chair, consultant, executive coach and strategist. Dr. Briscoe holds a Ph.D. in Executive Leadership and is also a Gallup-certified Strengths Coach and MBTI Certified Coach. Dr. Briscoe co-authored the Amazon Best Seller, Brave Women at Work—Lessons in Leadership.

Outside of the office, Dr. Briscoe is actively involved in promoting positive and sustainable community change through board service in the following organizations: President Loyola University—Women's Leadership Academy Alumni Advisory, 826 New Orleans (Immediate Past President), 826 National, Parent Leadership Training Institute—Civic Design Team, Teach for America Alumni Advisory (Co-Chair), and Faculty Women of Color in the Academy Advisory. She's excited to be named President-Elect Loyola University's Women's Leadership Academy Advisory.

She is happily married and has two beautiful children. Ronicka and her family currently reside in New Orleans, Louisiana.

In Relentless Pursuit of…
UPENDING THE UNICORN EFFECT

BY
RONICKA BRISCOE

IN THIS BOOK, YOU WILL READ STORIES OF INCREDIBLE WOMEN who are in *Relentless Pursuit* of self while Unapologetically Upending the Unicorn Effect. They are boldly challenging, disrupting, and redefining the narrative surrounding the unique and often isolating experiences of Black women.

Unapologetically Upending the Unicorn Effect involves Black women reclaiming power and identity. We embrace our intersectional identities without apology and reject the need to conform to societal or organizational expectations that marginalize or silence our authentic selves. We celebrate the complexity of being a Black woman as a strength rather than a burden.

We seek to break down barriers and dismantle systemic biases and oppressive structures that perpetuate inequality. We challenge stereotypes, microaggressions, and the "tokenism" often associated with being the only Black woman in the room.

We have redefined traditional leadership standards. Often leadership is looked at through the lens of formal professional leadership roles. Historically, we have not been given such roles, however we have continued to lead. We are shifting the paradigm of what leadership looks like by incorporating diverse perspectives, cultural values, and unique approaches to problem-solving; and redefining leadership through the multifaceted roles Black women play in their homes, in their families, communities and their lives more broadly: including motherhood and matriarchal duties. We see leadership through the eyes of Black women that honor resilience, authenticity, and the lived experiences of Black women.

Through writing autoethnographies, Black women's voices will be amplified and community will be built. These women will share personal stories and we hope you will create space to do the same, fostering a sense of solidarity and collective empowerment.

We are using the story as a form of resistance, refusing to settle for the status quo and challenging the notion that Black women must work harder to be seen as equal, rejecting the pressure to "prove" their worth. Advocating for systemic change that ensures equity, inclusion, and belonging in our families, communities, and professional spaces.

Writing and publishing these narratives is more than just sharing experiences—it's about leaving a legacy of change. We are paving the way by rejecting historical measures of success and creating our own opportunities to make history.

To unapologetically upend the Unicorn Effect is to lean into courage, authenticity, and resilience, reshaping societal expectations in a way that centers the unique strengths and contributions of Black women. It's a call to reject invisibility, silence, or compromise, and instead, lead with purpose, pride, and unapologetic self-acceptance.

IN RELENTLESS PURSUIT OF ME THROUGH AN AUTOETHNOGRAPHIC LENS

Through an autoethnographic lens, this book represents a deeply reflective and analytical exploration of personal experiences in the context of larger cultural, social, and systemic frameworks.

Autoethnography is more than just research—it's a powerful act of self-reflection and storytelling. It allows us to examine our lived experiences through a broader cultural and societal lens, connecting the personal to the systemic. Unlike traditional ethnography, where researchers study others, autoethnography positions us as both the subject and the analyst, giving voice to perspectives often overlooked. It's a tool for challenging dominant narratives, reclaiming our stories, and shaping the way history is written.

The following autoethnographic explorations by eight Black women emphasize:

1. Connecting the Personal to the Collective: The pursuit of self-discovery is not just an individual journey but is influenced by cultural narratives, societal expectations, and historical contexts. This lens allows the writer to critically examine how their unique experiences as a Black woman intersect with broader themes such as race, gender, and systemic inequities.

2. Interrogating Societal Expectations and Norms: The journey involves uncovering how societal pressures shape self-perception, leadership style, and personal goals. Autoethnographic writing enables the writer to analyze moments where they defied stereotypes or broke free from limiting beliefs, offering insights into the collective experience of Black women.

3. Reclaiming Authenticity and Agency: This pursuit is about reclaiming agency over one's narrative, challenging imposed labels, and redefining success on one's own terms. Autoethnographic storytelling highlights the tensions between personal identity, cultural identity, family identity, and societal roles, allowing for a rich exploration of how authenticity (wholeness and clarity of self) is cultivated in the face of external pressures.

4. Healing and Transformation: Reflecting on past experiences through autoethnography reveals patterns of resilience, moments of healing, and personal growth. The lens helps connect individual healing to systemic challenges, showing how overcoming personal struggles contributes to stepping into who you have chosen to become.

5. Redefining Leadership and Legacy: The pursuit involves challenging traditional leadership paradigms and contributing to a new vision of what leadership looks like for Black women. Autoethnographic analysis provides a platform to document these transformative insights and inspire others to pursue leadership unapologetically and authentically.

Through this lens, *In Relentless Pursuit of Me* becomes a powerful framework for connecting personal narrative with systemic critique, ultimately contributing to a collective reimagining of identity and purpose.

WRITE YOUR STORY

In times like the present when it feels like the world is on fire, figuratively and literally it's important for us to retain our power, especially power over our own story. Writing your own story on your own terms is resistance. We invite all of you to think about writing your own autoethnography. You will naturally begin to reflect on your own lived experience.

Consider the following guiding questions:
- How have historical events or cultural movements influenced your personal and professional journey, both directly and indirectly?
- What cultural or societal expectations have impacted your personal and professional decisions?
- How do your challenges reflect systemic issues faced by Black women because you are both black AND a woman?
- What role has your family life and community played in shaping your values and definition of success?
- In what ways do your successes and struggles contribute to your "relentless pursuit of self"?

Use the organizer in the back of the book to organize your thoughts.

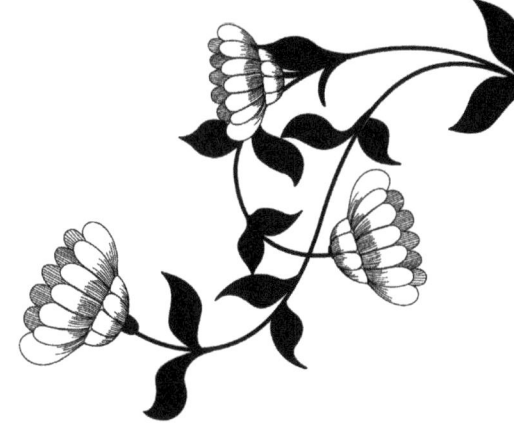

Introduction to
MONICA PIERRE

Monica Pierre is a three-time Emmy Award-winning reporter and producer, speaker, and Assistant Professor of Practice in the Mass Communication department at Xavier University of Louisiana in New Orleans, where she prepares the next generation of multimedia professionals for success in an ever-evolving media landscape.

Monica's on-air journey began during her college years and has landed her roles as a news reporter, radio and television host, and executive producer. Her accomplishments include three Emmy Awards, with her most recent honor recognizing her work as executive producer of *Battlegrounds: The Lost Community of Fazendeville*—a powerful documentary that recovered and amplified a story nearly lost to history.

Throughout her career, Monica has produced and hosted numerous talk shows, led in-depth coverage of significant news events, and brought attention to stories of resilience and transformation—including her reporting on the devastation and aftermath of Hurricane Katrina.

In Relentless Pursuit of…
MY VOICE

BY
MONICA PIERRE

"WHERE'S MONICA?!" His words ricocheted down the bright hallway.

I tensed, cocked my head, and held my breath. Ordinarily, interacting with unfamiliar people didn't put me on alert. Those interactions were usually brief, fun encounters with New Orleans radio station listeners who recognized my voice when I greeted them at the post office, grocery store, or local restaurant. These folks usually shared with me how much they enjoy hearing me on the air. Young Black girls, mothers, fathers, blue-collar workers, professionals, business owners, and elected officials often told me that my voice was warm, dignified, and comforting. Although not a New Orleans native, listeners and the city claimed me as one of their own.

These were not ordinary times. This was in the aftermath of Hurricane Katrina. Everyone was anxious, scared, uncertain, uncomfortable, suspicious, and angry. The local, state, and federal government let the people of New Orleans down. The world watched from a front-row seat and witnessed the devastation, disappointment, abandonment, and loss.

New Orleans flooded. Hundreds of thousands of residents—some with means and some with only what they could carry or load up in their vehicles—evacuated. Two days after the flooding, Katrina unleashed one-hundred-mile-per-hour winds, and the city was under water because of breached levees and slow response. Nothing would ever be the same.

Not everyone left. Some die-hard New Orleanians refused to allow storms, no matter how ferocious, to run them away. Too many didn't have the option of fueling their cars—they had no cars. They had no money and no way to get out. Many ended up in the Superdome or the Convention Center. The federal government and others took too long to get their response efforts together.

The levees broke. People drowned. Respondents rescued traumatized residents from the gathering places. Some were airlifted from their rooftops or overpasses in the blistering late-August sun. Those who fled for safety or were scattered around the country were called refugees, criminals, and "those New Orleans people."

My husband and I evacuated to Baton Rouge, eighty-two miles northwest of the city. My station was now part of United Radio Broadcasters of New Orleans. Thirteen stations owned by two media companies, Clear Channel (now iHeart Media) and Entercom Communications (now Audacy), banded together to run a single broadcast out of Baton Rouge. Clear Channel had the station well out of harm's way, and WWL/Entercom had the reach—a 50,000-watt transmitter and experienced talk show talent.

The New Orleans Clear Channel stations were music stations. What the on-air deejays lacked in news experience; they possessed a vested interest in getting the story right. They lived in New Orleans. It was their city underwater. Together, an on-air talent from each station would sit side-by-side, cover the crisis, and broadcast around the clock.

We weren't united. We were, at best, tolerated. But we were willing to put aside ratings and formats and put a unified front on the air.

I followed the sound of the voice requesting to see me, uncertain of the situation awaiting me. Was he upset? Why did he want to speak to me specifically? Did he hear something on the air that upset him? Was he searching for a loved one in the aftermath of Katrina and thought the radio station could help?

I rounded the corner and found the voice of the person asking for me; a twenty-something Black man with kind eyes. Although young his creased brow and tight mouth revealed the stress caused by the early days after the hurricane. Days and nights of covering the rescue, devastation, and the lagging recovery process probably appeared on my face too. I dipped my head and took a steeling breath in an attempt to hide my own fatigue.

"Hi, I'm Monica," I greeted him with a clear and steady voice.

"When I heard your voice on the air, I knew I could go on," he gushed and nearly fell into my arms.

Determined to tell me this news, he made his way to the upper floor of the station, disregarded suspicious eyes, and asked to see me.

He found me because he heard my voice. I didn't know him. He was desperate to let me know what my voice meant to him.

The Unicorn Effect is in the shadows, waiting for the moment to appear.

With this young man's eyes searching my countenance I battled my go-to reaction to compliments, which was to dismiss them. I marched to the drum of "do your work, cover your story, and then move quickly to the next." As a Black woman, I received messages early on that I didn't need praise or recognition for doing my job. My automatic instinct was to rush through this encounter and tell this man that while I appreciated him coming to the station, I was only doing my job.

But he was steadfast in his will to find and share with me, and I needed and wanted to be present and thankful. I rejected the authority and strength of the Unicorn Effect and embraced my power. I honored the connection with openness and authenticity.

"Thank you," I smiled and reached for his hand. "I am glad you found me and let me know what it meant to you."

We shook hands and nodded our understanding. Accepting who were and the importance of this shared moment.

As quickly as he arrived, he was gone, but his words are stored in my heart.

As Black women on-air talent or reporters, we are praised for being Unicorns while being dismissed and overworked, penalized for being bold, direct, or angry. We are often treated as an exception to the rule as long as we make others feel comfortable and we don't miss deadlines or fail to cover the stories. During my months at United Radio Broadcasters of New Orleans, we worked five-hour shifts at different times and days. There were no set schedules. Once, a producer commented that regardless of the time of day I was in the air, my voice never sounded tired. In her mind, it was meant as a compliment, but she also saw it as permission to schedule me any time, day or night, because I—my voice—could handle it. She never considered my need for rest.

In the 1990s and early 2000s in New Orleans, there were not impressive numbers of Black women reporters and anchors on television. One or two. Three or four, but eventually back to one or two. Even for a city like New Orleans, with an overwhelming majority Black population of sixty-six percent, I was often the "only one" or the one of a handful in the TV newsroom. While it would have been great to be a part of a mutually respectful community of Black women reporters, my overtures of wanting to get to know them better or create a bond were often met with skepticism.

Would my entry through the door mean they would eventually be shown the door? While the numbers of Black women in the newsrooms and on the air were starting to inch upward, the residue of systemic barriers and ingrained ideas from management and owners about who belonged, who had the look or the voice, and who would begrudgingly be allowed in, restricting these numbers from growing. Black women reporters and anchors were not as common as they should have been.

There is often no room for error or miscalculation for Black women on the air. You hold so much close to the vest out of the instinct for self-preservation. You don't have the option or luxury of being vulnerable. The expectation is that you will do what needs to be done. You will do it with excellence. That's expected.

The messages were clear to me. My voice was only used to do my job, not celebrate my gift, not to yell or scream or pitch a fit like so many of my white female reporters often did when things did not go their way, or they weren't assigned the stories they wanted to cover. I knew that I must be calm, reasonable, and ready to take on the next assignment without complaint or admission that I needed a break.

As Black women on the air, we move through the space and environment on guard because we know that the shoe can drop at any time. You could be out the door after your current contract ends. Or you could languish for years in the same position you started with, passed over for more desirable day parts or the anchor desks. Fellow reporters or editors who don't look like you or have the same shared life experiences or demands have no boundaries or problems approaching you with seemingly innocent ways to tap into your institutional knowledge, contacts, and wisdom. They need your help but never acknowledge or applaud you.

On the radio side of the industry, the Unicorn Effect plays out as Black women who typically aren't the lead hosts. Our names aren't mentioned first. We are in supporting roles—second bananas or the voice of reason. The morning and afternoon drive shows are mostly for male hosts, with women on-air talent relegated to mid-day, overnight, or weekend shifts, or, in my case, on the air as anchor, news director, and reporter, someone who had to "wear a lot of hats."

The pressures and expectations to learn your craft, get good at it, and use your voice to fight for the stories that need to be told, often lead to decisions that lean heavily on prioritizing and validating the needs of the many. Often those decisions come at the Black woman's expense. The Unicorn Effect influences what you say yes to. You put what *you* want on the back burner, biding your time. You take the job and money offered even when you know you deserve more. You hope for a payoff after you prove yourself.

One of my clearest examples of the Unicorn Effect came in the form of a new opportunity. It was a dream job! I would become part of a celebrated morning show team. I was pursued by the station's top executives who called me smart, knowledgeable, and a calming presence on the air. All the right things were said and promised. I was assured that I would be welcomed and regarded as part of the "station family."

Despite those assurances, I had reservations that I didn't verbalize. Many things didn't feel right, and I questioned if I really wanted the job. Ignoring my intuition and doubts I eventually agreed, this was an opportunity to make a difference in the community. The Unicorn Effect loves it when we play the martyr, when we are self-sacrificing. Do the right thing. Put others first.

I knew deep inside that I wanted to stop doing news and have my own show that was fun and positive. After years in news reporting, covering everything from hurricanes to homicides, I was ready for a change. Hard news and polarizing topics just for the sake of controversy didn't appeal to me.

I wanted to pivot and host my own motivational show. I knew it but disregarded what I wanted. I never even brought up a different show option during the interview with the station's management. I turned down the volume on my internal wisdom and turned up the voices that said I would be crazy to pass on what was being offered. Take it as is, I told myself. I was offered decent money. It's not about you; it's about the audience! Be the consummate professional. Eventually I would get the type of show I really wanted. The self-sacrifice would eventually be rewarded. Right?

There was no big announcement by the station letting the audience know I was joining the morning show. No red carpet. No news release. As the date of my official start neared, no one outside of my immediate family and close friends knew I was coming. It was as if it was a closely guarded secret. I told myself that I didn't need fanfare or a Mardi Gras parade. I would just show up. Smile. Do my job. It wasn't the first time I was expected to hit the ground running. It probably wouldn't be the last.

I didn't want to talk about the topics but acted as if I did. I didn't want to be the second banana on the show but acquiesced. Why hadn't I stood up for myself? I had let myself down again. This wasn't the first time I silenced my voice and accepted the first thing I was offered. When would I boldly and unapologetically pursue *me*? It was going to be a long three-year contract. This was only two weeks into the job!

Each time I stepped off the elevator, I sighed, and braced for another morning of putting on a brave face. I pretended with everyone. The audience. Management. Myself. I pretended it didn't matter that my co-host resented me and didn't want a partner.

It didn't take long before the cost of denying what I wanted and not using my voice started to take a physical toll on me. I developed stomach problems. I didn't want to go to work. For my entire career, I prided myself on pushing through no matter how I felt. In the past, I marched to work when I was ill, refusing to miss a single day.

Here I was calling in sick—a lot. Soon, my favorite day of the week, Sunday, was filled with dread and the evenings were the worst. I spent hours the night before my Monday-through-Friday on-air show anxious and wrestling the sheets without sleeping. I just didn't want to face another week. I couldn't. I knew that the audience was only getting some of me. I was getting none of me.

My time on the show did get better—or perhaps tolerable—over time. I found ways to bring elements of my authentic voice to the show, managing to provide more uplifting takes on topics. My decision not to renew my contract with the morning show opened the door for another opportunity—a different show at the station, one where I could use my voice to spotlight positive stories of organizations.

It never felt like work but an alignment. Finally, I was no longer pretending. I was pursuing *me*.

As an over sixty-year-old Black woman, there are more years behind me than in front of me. My life experiences—what I have said yes to and why I have put myself at the back of the line—have laid the foundation for recognizing that my voice has always been there; but I have not always shown up for my voice. There were times when I refused to listen to my own voice. There were times when I advocated for the community and became the voice of recovery and rebuilding. I've used my voice to utter words of encouragement. I am upending and embracing the Unicorn Effect by recognizing that it's not all or nothing.

I *can* be there for myself. I *can* be there for others. I *can* slow down and savor it. I *can* use my voice to create shows and interview the people I want to. I am the gatekeeper. When I catch myself rushing through a compliment from someone sharing what my voice means to them, I sit in the uncomfortableness of the moment. I allow the words of sincerity to fill me with gratitude. I know that being my voice takes patience and courage.

To be my voice means honoring that power, accepting it as a gift rather than a tool. It means rejecting the narrative that my worth is tied to my output. It means allowing myself to pause, relish moments of joy and recognition, and create on my own terms. I no longer see my voice as something I "use" for others. It is part of who I am—a reflection of my truth, my experiences, and my desires. It is my legacy.

August 29, 2025, marks twenty years since Hurricane Katrina hit the Gulf Coast and devastated the residents, culture, and washed away some of New Orleans's identity. The city is gentrified, with those who used to call it their home and neighborhood priced out and feeling voiceless. There will undoubtedly be countless hours of retrospect, analysis, and sadness at the losses and changes to a beloved city.

I often think of the young man whose words are still poignant. "When I heard your voice on the air, I knew I could go on."

When I get knocked off balance or aggravated by erroneous inner thoughts or systemic strongholds, I think of these words and how I heard and accepted them. The journey to being my voice is ongoing. There are moments of doubt when the Unicorn Effect threatens me with darkness.

I am committed to this pursuit. I am committed to showing up for myself, honoring my voice as a gift, and telling the stories that matter to me. This is my relentless pursuit—not just of success but of truth and acceptance.

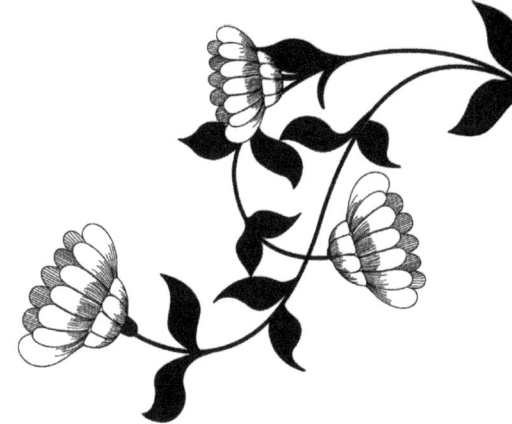

Introduction to
DOROTHY DOOLITTLE

Dr. Dorothy Doolittle is a nationally recognized education leader and presenter, specializing in helping state and district leaders build and implement sustainable systems that enhance educator effectiveness and student achievement. Raised in rural Arkansas in a large family, she experienced firsthand the obstacles faced by underserved communities. As one of the first in her family to earn a college degree and pursue advanced studies, Dorothy became a role model—proving that education is the gateway to opportunity and systemic change. Her life's work is dedicated to ensuring that all students, particularly those in historically marginalized communities, have access to high-quality learning experiences.

With over twenty years in education, Dorothy has led transformative initiatives that reimagine teaching, learning, and leadership at both the school and executive levels. Honored as Teacher of the Year and Math and Science Coach of the Year, she has empowered educators through impactful instructional strategies and systems. Her experience as a teacher, instructional coach, and administrator gives her deep insight into what educators need to thrive.

Leading large-scale teams of professional learning specialists, Dorothy drives systemic reform by guiding leaders in the development of sustainable instructional coaching models, coherent leadership frameworks, and curriculum implementation strategies. She has a track record for successfully spearheading multi-million-dollar initiatives focused on comprehensive school improvement, K-12 literacy, math and science, ensuring districts and agencies have the structures and tools necessary to improve educator capacity and student outcomes.

Dorothy's leadership extends beyond the classroom—she has served as Vice President of Strategic Partnership Solutions and Senior Executive Director of Professional Development, shaping professional learning standards and empowering thousands of educators. Her mastery of adult learning principles, data-driven decision-making, and leadership development has set a new standard for instructional excellence. As a sought-after consultant, she works closely with state and local leaders to implement policy, align professional learning, instructional improvement, and leadership development into sustainable, scalable frameworks that create lasting impact.

Currently serving as a consultant, Dorothy remains dedicated to helping leaders develop and implement customized strategies that meet the unique needs of their educational systems. She holds a doctorate in Educational Leadership and is a certified Organizational Development Coach. Dorothy continues to be a catalyst for innovation, ensuring that education leaders have the tools, knowledge, and systems to drive meaningful change for future generations.

When she's not making things happen professionally, you'll find her dedicating her time to meaningful volunteer work, orchestrating unforgettable parties, and indulging in the rich storytelling of period dramas. As a proud member of Delta Sigma Theta, Inc., she carries her passion for service and sisterhood wherever she goes. She shares her vibrant life with her devoted husband in the heart of Northwest Arkansas!

In Relentless Pursuit of
ENOUGHNESS

BY

DOROTHY DOOLITTLE

SOMETHING WAS WRONG.

It was time to get up, but my left eye refused to open. The side of my face felt weighted and swollen. Regardless, my brain raced to the day's to-do list—important meetings, travel plans, groceries. It didn't matter if I couldn't see, *I don't let interruptions derail a carefully planned schedule.*

I rolled out of bed and shuffled to the bathroom. I tried to catch a squinty glimpse of my reflection.

Who is that?

I straightened my stance to see what the full-length mirror said. The light pierced my brain, and I fought to focus. Both eyes resisted the light and my commands to open them. My face was the size of a melon. My left eye was sealed shut.

My 8:30 meeting loomed like an impossible mountain. How could I get camera-ready when I couldn't see, and I looked like this? A vice closed on my chest and my heartbeat raced. I sucked in a breath and contemplated my next move.

My husband, DJ, fully dressed in his gym gear, was in the other room gathering his things. I toyed with letting him leave while I figured things out, but I knew he would see my face when he came to kiss me goodbye. I had to ask for help.

"I can't see," I almost whispered, hoping he might not hear. My usually strong voice faltered with fear and frustration.

"What?!" DJ shouted and rushed back into the bedroom. His face screwed up with confusion when he saw me.

"Bells-Palsy?" he questioned.

The term meant nothing to me. No use in trying to look it up, I couldn't open my eyes, and with each effort the phone screen seared more pain into my head.

"What is that," I asked as I gave up on trying to read the AI-generated summary.

He started to explain but I dismissed it. Bells-Palsy comes with numbness.

"I doubt it," I quipped. "I can actually feel my face."

I wasn't laughing but I was pretending to not be worried.

"I will cancel my day," he said.

"No, I'm fine," I said with a clear and firm voice, imitating confidence. "I bet it's my allergies."

He paused, considering. He knew my tricks.

"Look, I'll call you if I need anything," I continued. "I promise."

I gave him a short nod and with the commitment to contact him he eventually relented. I didn't tell him about how much pain I was in. And I certainly didn't tell him about the fear dancing in my mind.

Alone. Alone with my fear and frozen eye. Worst-case scenarios took turns popping into my brain. *What would my colleagues think? How could I explain this?* The professional part of me rejected the idea of showing vulnerability, of admitting something was wrong. So, I adapted. Camera off. Apologetic messages. A performance of normalcy through audio calls.

I didn't tell anyone about my condition. I feared judgment would be swift and merciless. And I lied to myself and believed—hoped—this was just temporary and that it would pass. I just had to power through. I worked the whole day, with no one the wiser.

After a fitful night wrestling with my sheets, the next morning was no better. My left eye wept constantly, sluicing tears rolled down my face, and I there was no way to stop them. I faced down another 8:30 am meeting. Again, I retreated behind the safety of an audio connection, my camera a black screen, and my room shrouded in darkness. The curtains were drawn tightly to prevent even a speckle of light from filtering in. The light was my enemy.

The pain was a living thing. I tilted to the left as if this might offer some mysterious relief. Each movement was calculated, measured, and each breath a negotiation with my body's rebellion.

Inside I wasn't just managing a medical condition. I was fighting to maintain the narrative of control and perfection that I carefully constructed and lived by. My body was telling a story I wasn't ready to hear—a story of limits, vulnerability, and unexpected interruptions.

Little did I know then that this was just the beginning of a journey that would challenge everything I thought I knew about myself, about resilience, about the delicate balance between professional facade and human fragility. By the end of the second day, I knew I had to do something. My body was sending signals I couldn't and shouldn't ignore any longer.

During one of the many meetings of the day, one of my

colleagues, Charlotte, sent me a chat and joked, "It's unlike you to not be on camera looking fabulous." Something about her light-hearted comment broke through my wall of denial.

"It's my eye," I responded. "I can't see out of it for some reason. The light is hurting it so I'm off camera."

"Oh no," she quickly typed back. "Your body is trying to tell you to pull back. I bet it's stress!"

Stress? I scoffed. There was no way my eye would be closed due to stress. Her words chewed through the wall I built. Although I hadn't yet made a doctor's appointment, Charlotte's observation was a tiny seed of truth being planted in the fertile ground of my exhaustion.

I finally made an appointment, scheduling it strategically at the end of the day to minimize disruption to my work. Even in seeking medical help, I positioned myself to not inconvenience anyone. The darkness of my home was a manifestation of my internal state—a protective cocoon where I was momentarily hiding from the world's expectations.

The doctor's office was a stark contrast to my dimmed sanctuary. There were a handful of patients in the waiting room, and they seemed to be more in need than I, my issue was no big deal. I tried to appear cool, wearing black shades. However, under the clinical lights, my condition felt both more real and more vulnerable.

My wait was brief, the nurse took me to the small cubical room and asked a series of questions. The more questions she peppered at me the more irritated I became. I didn't know what was wrong! I didn't have a clear reason or explanation for what I was experiencing.

The doctor assessed my condition and explained that my eye was irritated, likely from excessive screen time and that I had damaged a nerve, a complex mix of emotions surged through me.

"You need to rest your eyes completely," he said. "I suggest three-to-four days of rest without screen time, but it may take longer." He handed me a jelly-like substance and instructed me to use it multiple times a day for a week and to return in a week to check on my progress.

I couldn't cry—the pain was too intense, too raw. But inside, a storm brewed. Rest? How could I possibly rest? There were meetings scheduled. Training sessions to deliver. And I knew my hard-driving boss wouldn't possibly ever understand.

Vulnerability was not an option. He was bound to run a shadow operation to malign me from my own project. Anytime he could see an opportunity to "help" he did. His kind of help typically meant a load of clean-up for me to do afterward.

No, I did not want his help.

It was as if I had lost my hearing too. "Wait, how much time do I need to take off?" I asked, my voice tight.

He smiled and restated his recommendations. The doctor's prescription was both literal and metaphorical—eye medication to provide physical relief, and an unspoken recommendation to address the deeper issue of my relentless pace.

As I walked to my car, I realized this was more than just a medical issue. This was my body's dramatic intervention, forcing me to confront the unsustainable rhythm of my life. The closed eye, the pain, the enforced darkness—they were all speaking a language I was too busy to hear.

Charlotte was right. I pushed myself beyond rational limits and was now at the mercy of mandatory rest. The irony wasn't lost on me—I who had always prided myself on being the ultimate support system was now completely exposed.

What would it take for me to truly listen? Losing my eyesight?

While I had been protecting my staff, constantly stepping in to cover mistakes, to make our team look good, to smooth over every potential rough edge, I was completely neglecting my own needs. And the most eye-opening realization? There was literally no one doing the same for me. At least, I hadn't allowed anyone to do so. I mean, I essentially kicked my husband out of the house when I couldn't even see! I built walls so high and created such an image of invincibility that I was isolated.

In retrospect, this wasn't the first time I'd pushed myself beyond human limitations, and if I was honest with myself, it probably wouldn't be the last. I seemed destined to learn important life lessons through painful, dramatic interventions from my own body.

Each time I overextended, each time I ignored the

whispers of exhaustion, ignored disrespect, my body would ultimately stage a revolt. This eye issue was just the latest chapter in a long story of self-neglect. I normalized overworking and turned martyrdom into a perverse form of professional pride. My worth, I decided, was measured by how much I could endure, how many fires I could put out, how many people I could save—even at the cost of saving myself.

The darkness of my room, the throbbing pain in my eye, the forced stillness were metaphorical mirrors. Reflecting back at me was a woman who had forgotten how to be human, who had transformed herself into a machine of productivity and self-protection.

Charlotte's words echoed in my mind: "Your body is trying to tell you to pull back." And now, forced into stillness, I was listening.

As I write this chapter, I'm aware of the complex layers that make up my journey as a Black woman in leadership. I seek to reach other Black women leaders who, like me, are still processing the residual effects of childhood abandonment—both its perceptions and its stark realities.

Through extensive counseling and deep self-reflection, I've confronted some hard truths. Some of these truths are about me, while others are about the people I love most—people who did their best with what was handed down to them. One of the hardest truths I've acknowledged is that I never felt like I was enough in any setting I occupied.

There has always been a persistent whisper that says, "You don't belong here." It's not just a thought but a weighty inheritance carried by Black women in professional spaces, a generational millstone that sits between our shoulder blades, pressing down with each step we take.

The irony is not lost on me. Black women are among the most educated demographic in the workplace, our credentials meticulously gathered, our expertise carefully cultivated. And yet, the imposter syndrome lingers as an unwelcome shadow, constantly threatening to expose us as frauds.

When an opportunity arrives—rare and precious as it is—we don't just step into the role. We launch ourselves, full force, into it determined to dismantle every stereotype, every limiting narrative about Black womanhood. We aren't just working; we are performing a complex choreography of excellence, proving not just our individual worth, but rewriting collective narratives.

This isn't just about personal success. This is about representation. This is about creating space where none was originally intended for us.

So we dig our heels in. We work harder. We work smarter. We anticipate every possible critique before it's spoken. We become so good they can't ignore us, so precise they can't doubt us. We transform ourselves into living rebuttals of every negative trope about Black women in professional spaces.

But this constant performance comes at a cost. We are overextended, our boundaries blurred, and our sense of self lost in the relentless pursuit of proving our worth. We are simultaneously the most valuable and the most undervalued—our labor celebrated yet rarely compensated, our excellence acknowledged yet rarely appropriately rewarded.

Burnout isn't just a possibility. It is inevitable.

I think about the generations of Black women who came before me, who didn't have the opportunities, who fought so we could be in these rooms. Their spirits ride with me, pushing me forward, reminding me that my presence is not just personal, but political.

We are not just working. We are creating pathways. We are healing generational wounds. We are reconstructing professional landscapes that were never designed with our humanity in mind.

The work continues. Not because we must prove our worth, but because we know our worth is inherent, regardless of external validation.

From the moment I understood my place in the world, I was conditioned to prove my worth. I am the eighth child of a family of sixteen children, a number that speaks to complexity, to abundance, to a life of constant negotiation. But my story is not about the multitude of siblings, but about the singular journey of being chosen—or perhaps, separated.

My aunt and uncle provided me a life of comfort and opportunity that was both miraculous and precarious. They gave me access to resources I might never have known, but their provision came with an unspoken contract: I must be exceptional.

Always.

As an inquisitive child who constantly asked *why*, I couldn't reconcile the most fundamental question of my existence: Why me? Why was I the only child selected to live with them, pulled from the large tapestry of my biological family? The absence of a clear answer became my first lesson in navigating uncertain belonging.

This uncertainty became a survival strategy, where perfection became my shield against displacement. I could not make myself fully at home because my existence felt temporary and conditional—something I had to constantly justify through meticulous performance. Good grades weren't achievements but evidence of my worth; staying out of trouble wasn't just behavior but a demonstration that my presence wasn't a mistake. These childhood dynamics created the blueprint for my professional persona, where every project became an opportunity to validate my existence and every task a chance to prove I deserved the space I occupied.

My upbringing served as a masterclass in navigating systemic marginalization, teaching me that for Black women, excellence isn't optional but necessary. The high expectations from my aunt and uncle were preparing me for a world that would question my right to occupy certain spaces. My childhood taught me that belonging isn't a birthright but something to be earned, negotiated, and constantly defended—a lesson that followed me into every professional environment where my value would be measured by my output and my ability to exceed expectations.

Every achievement became an extension of those childhood performances: proving my worth, justifying my existence, and showing that I was not a mistake. Therefore, in my career, I was not just working. I was continually proving my right to be there.

One summer, my team was tasked with organizing and facilitating a large-scale professional development for thousands of teachers K-5. A multi-million dollar project that expanded our organization's reach to grades sixth through eighth. On paper, it looked like an opportunity. In reality, it was a gauntlet designed to test every ounce of my professional resilience.

From the beginning, every request I made was met with systematic resistance. Resources? Denied. Meeting spaces? Unavailable. Direct client communication? Blocked. Content review? Dismissed. When I raised concerns about the training materials lacking engagement, I was told I didn't understand the program well enough. My expertise my professional experience—all insufficient and invisible.

But invisibility was never my default setting, nor did I accept it.

What they didn't see was the invisible labor: the countless hours of strategic recalibration, the sleepless nights reconstructing what should have been supported. While being told *no* at every turn, I was finding ways to say *yes* to the project's success.

Four and a half weeks away from my family. Two weeks of intense preparation, two weeks of on-site training, three days of post-project cleanup. Each moment was a silent rebellion against a system designed to make me fail.

When the client spoke highly of the sessions, it wasn't just a professional victory. It was a statement. A declaration that excellence transcends institutional barriers.

My boss's casual, "Wow, you pulled it off…" I recognized as a backhanded compliment. But I knew the truth. This wasn't about "pulling it off." This was a precise execution. This was leadership. This was a transformation.

"No," I stated. "I executed a plan."

In that moment, I wasn't just delivering a project. I was dismantling expectations. I was rewriting narratives about Black women's professional capabilities. Every *no* I encountered became a strategy, every barrier a challenge to be strategically navigated.

The unspoken narrative here is survival. Not just professional survival, but the survival of dignity. The ability to excel not just despite obstacles, but by transforming those obstacles into opportunities for excellence.

It was never clear to me what my boss was hoping for. He either wanted to see me sweat or fail. He made it known to both my colleagues and direct reports that he lacked confidence in my process. Instead of drowning, I showed him how rivers are made—persistent, powerful—carving new paths through seemingly immovable landscapes. I revealed what it looks like when expertise, experience, and resourcefulness meet opportunity: a force of nature that doesn't announce its strength but simply transforms everything in its path, reshaping the very terrain that once tried to contain it.

The weekend after the project was not a celebration. It was a collapse.

From Friday to Monday, I wasn't alive. Bed-bound, unmoving, existing in a fog of exhaustion. My body, which had carried me through weeks of intense work—lifting boxes in heels, ripping tape, coordinating massive logistical challenges—refused to move. My stiff limbs were only matched by my emotional devastation.

Why was I denied resources? What did I do wrong? Did I make my team proud? Is the team proud of the work we did? Did we really do a great job, or am I being delusional? These questions echoed through my restless sleep, and relentless internal interrogation of my worth.

I couldn't shake the stress of not knowing the answer to the bank of questions I had compiled, so I called my therapist, Dr. Cooper.

During my visit, I tearfully poured out my heart. As I was finally slowing down, I looked to him for the answers to my questions. I was seeking his praise, empathy, and validation. But what I noticed was a furrowed brow. He simply looked at me with eyes that had witnessed this pattern a hundred times before.

"You're doing it again," his deep metered voice replied. "You tried to do it all. You're trying to carry the ocean in cupped hands."

"I had no other choice," I retorted. "The team was

counting on me, and students need good instruction!"

"You had the choice to document the limitations, list the risks, and let the organization get you the help you needed to do your job."

His stare relentless, he went on, "So, tell me, what were you really trying to prove?"

His words crystallized and I recognized the connection. I had the answer to his question, but shame came over me, and I dismissed the probe with a shake of my head.

We sat in silence.

The little girl who was never sure why she was chosen, who had to be perfect to justify her existence, was still very much present in my professional self. I wasn't just executing a project; I was continuing to prove my worth, to show that I deserved to be in that space. The multi-million dollar project, the sleepless nights, the physical breakdown—they were all symptoms of a deeper narrative.

Dr. Cooper's words were an invitation to acknowledge and embrace a different way of existing. Not through constant proving, but through sustainable excellence. Not by breaking myself to meet impossible standards, but by recognizing my inherent worth.

This wasn't just about professional development or project management. This was about unlearning generations of survival strategies, about redefining success on my own terms.

I returned to work with a chip on my shoulder and a suffocating sense of isolation that seemed to follow me.

Weeks following the event, the loss of my biological mother, Brenda, bombed my carefully constructed truce with work. The grief and workplace tension collided, creating a volatile mix of emotions I wasn't prepared to navigate.

Dealing with the passing of my bio-mom, I found myself in a familiar pattern—performing strength, denying vulnerability, and being caught between worlds.

Because I didn't grow up in her house, I convinced myself that my grief was illegitimate. Every tear felt like a betrayal to my aunt and uncle who had given me so much. I compartmentalized my emotions. I was there for my siblings, a pillar of support, while carefully dissociating from my own sadness.

Our relationship defied traditional mother-daughter narratives. Brenda wasn't the mother who raised me, but our connection was undeniable, especially as I grew older. In my adult years, I developed a deep empathy for her. I wanted to know her story, to understand the woman behind the mother. But she wasn't one to really share—at least not with me. Perhaps we both had that trait, that careful guarding of our inner worlds.

The questions I never asked her haunted me. The *whys* that lingered between us remained unspoken, though I knew pieces of her story. We shared something profound—a hunger for maternal love that neither of us fully understood or received. It was an invisible thread connecting our experiences across generations.

Her home was the antithesis of my aunt and uncle's

structured environment. There were no rules, just endless adventure and laughter. It was a place where a rotating cast of characters shared stories that scandalized my aunt. Visiting Brenda's home provided a necessary balance in my life—showing me different ways of being, of loving, of living.

At her funeral, I witnessed a side of her I sensed but never fully grasped. Person after person stood to speak about her heart of gold, about how she provided refuge in their darkest moments. Young and old alike shared stories of her generosity, her supportive nature, and her ability to create safe spaces for others.

In many ways, she was like me—or perhaps I was like her. We both found purpose in supporting others, in creating spaces where people felt seen and valued. But while she did it with an open heart and infectious laughter, I learned to do it through performance and perfection.

The irony wasn't lost on me. Here I was, struggling to acknowledge my own grief while simultaneously maintaining my professional facade of competence and control. My mother lived authentically, offering support freely, while I turned support into a carefully choreographed performance of excellence.

My identity was shaped in the space between two mothers—one who gave me life and one who gave me opportunity. This duality created a specific emotional architecture within me. From my aunt, I inherited the drive for excellence, the understanding that opportunities must be earned through impeccable performance. From my biological mother, though less directly, I learned about the raw authenticity of giving, even when your own cup isn't full.

The complexity of loving two mothers of belonging everywhere and nowhere simultaneously, taught me to be adaptable but never fully present. In professional spaces, this translated into being everyone's support system while maintaining careful emotional distance. Like my biological mother, I was known for taking care of others, but unlike her authentic giving, mine came wrapped in layers of perfectionism and performance.

My maternal relationships taught me that love and worth were somehow tied to utility—what you could provide, how well you could perform, how much you could endure. It's no wonder that in my professional life, I consistently took on impossible tasks, pushed beyond reasonable limits, and measured my value by my ability to overcome systemic barriers through sheer force of will and creativity. This was the inheritance of my complex maternal relationships—the constant dance between authenticity and performance, between giving and proving, between being and becoming.

Yet, in the midst of unacknowledged and unprocessed bereavement, the landscape of my professional life was shifting. Months had passed and before I realized it, I whipped through four bosses in two years. My reputation shadowed me—"high performer, but different." The coded language wasn't lost on me. Being "different" in corporate spaces often meant being Black, being woman, being from out of the region, being from a different culture, depending on who was doing the measuring.

"I don't always know what she is thinking," they said about me.

The irony was bitter—I spent years making myself transparent through performance, through excellence, through over-delivery, and still, I remained inscrutable to them.

The infantilization began subtly. People whom I perceived to once respect my expertise now spoke to me as if I were a junior employee. The final indignity came with my next huge multi-million dollar project—I was told to report to a part-time sales person. The disrespect was palpable, but more painful was the lack of support when I sought help. My new boss's advice to "just do what they want" and HR's silence spoke volumes about the institutional dynamics at play.

Dr. Cooper's words echoed in my mind: "Say what you need and share the risks."

But grief and ego had formed an alliance within me, clouding my judgment. Instead of following his wisdom, I chose the familiar path of proving my worth through resistance and excellence. After all, wasn't I the only one who had successfully managed projects of this scale in my department?

But this time was different. My strategy, born from a combination of professional wounds and personal grief, created chaos instead of order. The delicate structure I had built—my reputation for excellence, my place in the hierarchy, my carefully cultivated professional relationships—began to crack under the weight of accumulated stress.

This was the last straw. A new client was asking for support, and during a coaching conversation, they revealed they wanted more than what was initially presented and were open to other modalities of service delivery. Following my instincts as a coach, I sent an email to a senior salesperson, asking if he would consider another approach to supporting the client.

His response was public mockery in that email chain, witnessed by ten colleagues. When no one came to my defense, I understood the reality of my isolation. My relentless need to prove my worth had inadvertently pushed away potential allies. The social capital I thought I had built through performance had evaporated like morning dew under a harsh sun.

In that moment of public humiliation, I felt the echo of childhood abandonment—that familiar sensation of being alone in a room full of people who were supposed to care. The professional became deeply personal, each word in that email striking not just at my work but at the core of who I believed myself to be. I waited two days for someone—anyone—to acknowledge what had happened, to offer even the smallest gesture of support. The silence was deafening. The weight of it all was unbearable, and I resigned. Not as an act of surrender, but as the first step toward reclaiming my worth beyond what I could produce or endure.

Submitting my resignation wasn't just about leaving a job and a hefty salary. It was about acknowledging that the patterns I developed to survive—the constant proving, the relentless performance, the isolation in excellence—had finally turned against me. In trying to prove I couldn't be denied resources and respect again, I denied myself the very support system I needed!

The decision was both liberation and loss. In gaining my freedom, I had to admit that I had lost control—something I'd spent a lifetime maintaining. It was a costly lesson in the price of proving, in the exhaustion of excellence, in the loneliness of being "different."

To add insult to injury, as my aunt would say, the same boss who had labeled me "different" and "difficult," the same leader who had maintained a deafening silence when a powerful male colleague publicly humiliated me, now approached me with a proposition that revealed the depths of her misunderstanding. She asked, with what I imagine was a performative tone of professional courtesy, if I would be interested in staying on as a consultant.

I remember the moment coalescing around me—my past self would have been desperate to prove her wrong, to show my value, to accept any crumb of professional recognition. But in that moment, something profound had shifted. I looked her directly in the eye and said with absolute clarity, "No, I am not interested in staying as a consultant."

My response was not angry, not defensive—it was a complete statement of my own worth. In her casual ask, she had inadvertently exposed how little she truly saw me—not as a valued professional, but as a disposable resource to be reconfigured at her convenience. And in that moment, I chose myself completely, walking away not with bitterness, but with a radical act of self-preservation.

After leaving, the familiar internal voices of unworthiness grew louder. In my darkest moments, I convinced myself that I had proven them all right—that somehow, my departure validated every doubt, every microaggression, every moment of isolation. The weight of perceived failure settled heavily on my shoulders, triggering a depressive episode.

But this time was different.

Perhaps it was the culmination of everything—the physical exhaustion from proving, the emotional toll of my mother's loss, the professional humiliation, the patterns Dr. Cooper tried to help me see. This breakdown wasn't just another cycle of depression; it was my body, mind, and spirit collectively saying *enough*.

In the depths of this depression, I made another visit to Dr. Cooper. This time, my visit focused on revelations and solutions, not to wallow in self-pity. I finally began to understand and allowed myself to see. My worth wasn't tied to my ability to endure impossible circumstances. My value wasn't measured by how much I sacrificed. The constant need to prove myself wasn't just a professional strategy—it was a wound from childhood still bleeding into my adult life.

The real progress came when the pattern was revealed to me: the chosen child becoming the chosen professional, always performing, always proving, never quite believing I deserved to simply be. My biological mother's passing cracked open something in me—a recognition that like her, I was giving from an empty cup, creating refuge for others while remaining homeless in my own heart.

This breakthrough didn't come as a lightning bolt of clarity, but as a slow, measured awakening. The very thing I feared—losing control, appearing vulnerable, admitting I couldn't do it all—was the key to my transformation. In failing to prove them wrong, I finally proved to myself that I was worthy of rest, of support, of choosing my own definition of success.

For the first time, I wasn't just surviving my depression; I was letting it teach me about my own humanity.

Through therapy and deep reflection, I began to understand that my worth wasn't a performance to be proven but a truth to be lived. The transformation started with small acts of radical self-acceptance.

I learned to say *no* without a dissertation of justification. To ask for help without feeling like a failure. To accept that my expertise didn't require constant validation through superhuman feats of endurance. These weren't just professional strategies; they were acts of self-love that directly challenged my programming of conditional worth.

This wasn't just healing; it was revolution. A personal revolution that changed how I showed up in every space—not as someone seeking validation through performance, but as someone who knew her worth was non-negotiable.

The challenges didn't disappear with my newfound awareness. The expectations for Black women in leadership remained just as demanding, the systemic barriers just as real, the pressure to prove just as present. But something fundamental shifted in how I met these challenges.

I began to recognize the early warning signs of slipping into old patterns. When I felt that familiar urge to over-function, to sacrifice my well-being for organizational success, to prove my worth through martyrdom disguised as servant leadership, I paused. I became better equipped to check myself before crossing that line between meaningful contribution and self-destruction. Self-checking became a crucial ritual of self-preservation in those moments:

- When asked to take on additional responsibilities without additional resources
- When expected to fix systemic problems through individual effort
- When faced with the subtle invalidation of my expertise
- When pressured to represent all Black women through my performance
- When my physical health was at risk

Instead of automatically rising to these challenges through personal sacrifice, I learned to respond with strategic boundaries. Yes, I remained committed to excellence, but not at the cost of my well-being. Yes, I continued to lead and serve, but not from a place of proving my right to exist in these spaces.

The most powerful change wasn't in how others treated me, but how I treated myself. The voice that once pushed me toward literal blindness and burnout in the name of service now reminded me that true leadership includes modeling healthy boundaries and sustainable excellence.

I acknowledge the deep impact of generational trauma on my life, especially feelings of abandonment.

- I draw strength from my ancestors who endured significant hardships and passed their resilience to me.
- "Follow peace with all men, and holiness, without which no man will see the Lord." (Hebrews 12:14, shared by my sister-cousin Vickie)
- I commit to breaking unhealthy cycles by setting uncommon but necessary boundaries.
- I will continue seeking personal therapy and support for emotional healing and growth.
- I choose to build and nurture relationships that sustain me.
- I remember that ego simply means "Edging GOD Out."
- I embrace that it's okay not to be perfect—I am already enough.

My swollen eye forced me into darkness, my body's desperate attempt to make me stop and see what I had been missing. In those early days of excruciating pain, I existed in a half-world of shadows, taking calls with the camera off, pushing through agony because stopping wasn't an option in my personal calculus of worth.

I literally couldn't see what was happening to me, couldn't recognize the patterns destroying me from within. My body had to shut down one sense to awaken another, more essential one, as systemic pressures convinced me my worth was tied to my ability to endure, my childhood wounds creating the perfect foundation for professional martyrdom, my inheritance as a Black woman conditioned to be impossibly strong at my own expense.

Now, years later, I face challenges with both eyes open, distinguishing between meaningful service and self-destructive sacrifice, between responding to present needs and reacting to past wounds. The journey from blindness to sight wasn't linear—it required confronting painful truths about my upbringing, my professional patterns, and my internalized beliefs about worth. But now I stand clear-eyed, seeing myself with compassion when old patterns emerge, perceiving the complete landscape of what's being asked of me, what I can genuinely offer, and what I must protect.

The eye that once closed in protest has given me a new way of seeing—not just physical sight, but the profound vision that comes from honoring one's whole self. In losing sight temporarily, I gained a vision that will never again allow me to become blind to my own humanity.

I am enough.

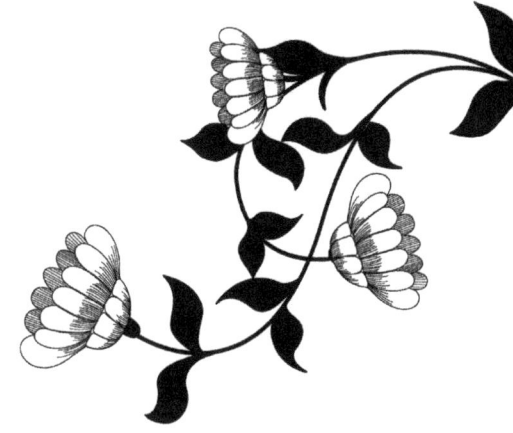

Introduction to
AARON HARRISON

Born and raised on the Westbank of New Orleans, Louisiana, Ms. Aaron Harrison is a proud two-time honor graduate of Xavier University of Louisiana. She earned a Bachelor of Science degree in Biology-Pre Med and later a Master of Arts in Teaching, solidifying her passion for education and lifelong learning.

Ms. Harrison has always been an avid reader and an enthusiastic learner. Her love for science and literature, coupled with her commitment to increasing literacy in her community, naturally led her to pursue a career in teaching. For nearly thirteen years, she has served as a dedicated Science and Special Education teacher, working with students from elementary through 12th grade.

Beyond the classroom, Ms. Harrison embraces her vibrant New Orleans culture. She enjoys touring her city, visiting museums, attending festivals, and exploring the French Quarter on her electric scooter with her family. Her deep love for her community inspired her to co-found the Legacy Foundation for Girls, a nonprofit organization aimed at empowering young women and fostering future leaders.

Ms. Harrison's dedication to education, community engagement, and personal growth continues to leave a lasting impact on the lives of her students and her community.

In Relentless Pursuit of
AUTONOMY

BY
AARON HARRISON

GRANDMA'S BABY—MY ROOTS RUN DEEP

"Lulabelle!"

"Huh?"

"I need you to go upstairs, light my cigarette, brung me my beeeer and come move these 'ya chairs so I can mop the floor. Ya heard dat?"

"Okay Bigmama."

At three years old, I knew the routine. Mama already left for work and my aunt was dropping off my sister and cousin at school. It was just me and my Bigmama. She is a New Orleans grandmother through and through. Bigmama cooked, cleaned, gossiped, drank beer and smoked cigarettes all day. I followed her closely enough that I could be mistaken for her shadow. I trailed behind her and never uttered more than a word or two in response to her commands.

"My Lou. Turn on my stories, please. I gotta iron that man shirt and cook something devil-ishous this evening."

I scurried to turn on the old television perched on the floor. It had a deformed knob that required pliers to change the channel. The makeshift antenna was a wire hanger with an aluminum foil cover. Even turning on the TV could be challenging, but I was just as invested as she was to see what sort of mess, drama, or romance would be brewing on "The Young and the Restless," followed by "The Bold and The Beautiful," "As the World Turns," and "The Guiding Light." The neurons in my young brain were firing as I moved through the day completing chores. I wiped down furniture, dried wet dishes by hand, and folded warm towels fresh from the dryer. I took pride in building my own "Thomas the Train" by aligning rows of dining chairs while the soap operas droned on in the background.

Growing up in New Orleans, Louisiana wasn't always as easy as the city's nickname claims. My mother was a single parent working two jobs to support two kids. Like many of my classmates in the city, we were being raised by our grandmas while our single mothers toiled away at minimum wage. My grandmother gladly took on the added responsibility of caring for me while also caring for her husband, ten children, and countless other grandchildren and extended family members. We lived in a two-story townhouse in a community that was one step away from being "the projects." I understood at a young age that it wasn't always safe outdoors, and my fun would have to come from within: within myself and within the walls of Bigmama's house and all the people in it.

By the time I came along in the late 1980's, I was not only my mother's baby but the baby of the entire family and two years younger than my sister and cousin. I got to have Bigmama all to myself before I started school. In those critical years of rapid growth and development, I taught myself to read. And I read any and everything I got my hands on, from my grandma's copy of *The Holy Bible*, to *The Real Yellow Pages* and *Reader's Digest*. While exploring the corridors of my childhood home, I built an imagination fantastical enough to rival Mr. Rogers and I developed an insatiable thirst for knowledge. These magical years shaped my identity and many of my core beliefs like *family first*, *knowledge is power*, and *happiness comes from within*.

Regardless of my surroundings, or maybe because of them, I got a head start in discovering myself. More importantly, I found happiness and joy as a lone wolf, always connected to the pack, but capable of surviving on my own. So now when people ask me how it is that I came to be so uniquely different from literally every person in my huge family; how I'm quietly observant instead of boisterously outspoken, how I'm helpful without expecting anything in return, how I'm intelligent and creative with a carefree spirit, how I am not beholden to the success-driven demands of a capitalist society, and a how I became a nonconformist brave enough to navigate through life as a single, childless, financially independent woman; I tell them it all began with my grandma, whom I lovingly call Bigmama. My never-ending search for *self* begins with her and set the stage for my *relentless pursuit of me*.

MILITARY RAISED ME—ADAPTING TO MY SURROUNDINGS

My mom married my step-father when I was eight years old. He was a Lance Corporal in The United States Marine Corps. As with all military service members, the time came when he was required to leave New Orleans and report for duty at Camp LeJeune Marine Corps Base in North Carolina. I was totally fine with him leaving. I never dreamed he'd have to take my mom, my sister and me with him! Yikes! Besides my sister and mom, my grandma and cousin were my entire world. I wondered how I would survive in a place where Bigmama wouldn't be there. Who would cook breakfast, lunch and dinner? Who would mop the floors and let the soap operas chatter in the background of our lives?

I most certainly didn't want to leave my cousin, who was my best friend since birth. We were the Black girl version of The Three Musketeers: my sister, my cousin, and me. We attended the same school and spent every day together, before and after school. My girls were the reason I didn't want or need other friends at school. Although I credit myself and my grandma with a lot of my early, advanced brain development, I cannot deny the influence of the two girls, now women, who blazed the trail before me.

Our nicknames were an insight into our personalities. My sister was "The Professor." She was the oldest, two months older than my cousin, and she commanded our obedience like a second mother. She taught us everything she learned in school. At home, she'd make us sit as if we were The Knights of the Round Table, and she was King Arthur. When she read to us, we were expected to recall every detail of *Danny and the Dinosaur*.

My cousin was "The Red Ant." A rebel and firecracker. She was the same age as my sister but joined me in frivolous play and laughter every time The Professor's back was turned. She led by example in her own way, and taught me to wing it when necessary, take risks now and worry about the consequences later, and how to find the humor in even the bleakest of situations.

I was "Mother Owl," wise beyond my years and the fulcrum providing balance to the seesaw of two extremes: the strict, disciplined, goal-oriented "Professor" and the rebellious, free-spirited, comedic "Red Ant." What was once an inseparable whole, would now be a disbanded team, scattered among states, retaining only our rough edges as evidence of our past selves.

Everything about living in North Carolina was a culture shock. No one else at school looked like me or talked like me. Gone were the days of raucous classrooms filled with laughter and New Orleans slang. No more gossiping with classmates, braiding each other's hair, and planning sleepovers. No more whole-group adventures at recess playing tag, hopscotch, double dutch, Little Sally Walker, and Mickey Mouse Built a House.

In New Orleans, I started Pre-K at four years old, and being around that many strangers was uncomfortable for me, especially after years of being alone with Bigmama and the soap opera characters. Early on the North Carolina teachers, like the teachers in New Orleans, Louisiana (NOLA), recognized that I was a gifted student, and my quiet observant nature allowed me to fly under the radar. Later, being introverted helped with the stark transition to the Department of Defense (DOD) schools in North Carolina. I settled into these new environments, simply by being intelligent and inconspicuous.

I was a master chameleon, adapting and blending in seamlessly whenever the environment changed. There was a part of me that felt like at this new school I was betraying my roots and culture from back home, but another part of me finally felt seen and acknowledged. Here my hunger for knowledge was fed abundantly.

I was in the Accelerated Reader program where I fell in love with science fiction and fantasy novels. In the Gifted program, I accessed computers long before any of my peers back home. I learned keyboard typing, website coding, using a floppy disc, and eventually a CD. The highlight of my week was playing Oregon Trail. I starred as Helena in the school's production of William Shakespeare's *A Midsummer Night's Dream*. I was featured in a local magazine for kids celebrating how I was benefiting from the lasting impact of Martin Luther King Jr.'s fight for equality. I question now if I *was* in fact reaping the benefits from his work.

Oftentimes as the only Black girl in my class, I was ignored and excluded from social conversations. I outsmarted everyone on the educational front, but when it came to trending pop culture, storytelling, and socializing, I was the observer—Mother Owl. Some of it, well a lot of it, was inane drivel that did not interest me anyway because what they talked about was nothing like the conversations I had with my NOLA friends.

These kids had no clue what it was like to listen to Bounce music or Second Line Jazz while eating a twenty-five-cent, Kool-Aid infused cold cup and pickled okra on the front porch. Those kids didn't know what it was like to come to school and cry over a relative getting shot or ending up in jail. I never heard talk of their lights being cut off or using food stamps at the store or having to eat nasty ol' commodity cheese.

To be fair, I couldn't relate to their stories of Disney World or camping trips. I'd never been to the circus or any professional sporting events. My celebrity crushes weren't Brad Pitt and Leonardo Dicaprio. My parents didn't take us to restaurants or bring us to Chuck-e-Cheese. I was always comparing myself to them, and even though I was gifted and smart, I still didn't feel good enough.

HIGH SCHOOL HELL—FINDING LIGHT IN THE DARKNESS

In high school we moved again. I was comfortable, and even enjoying North Carolina and I hated to leave before my eighth-grade graduation. But I was excited to return to Louisiana. I hadn't heard of Lafayette, Louisiana but since it was only a two-and-a-half-hour drive away from New Orleans, I figured it would be the same. I couldn't have been more wrong!

Lafayette was Cajun country and nothing like the Black, Creole culture I relished in New Orleans. They spoke a broken Cajun French dialect that was foreign to me. My name wasn't "Cher" or "Sha" but they called me that at every turn.

"Aww, may sha! Where ya from my gul? Ya talk White yea, yuh know?"

"Uhhh, I'm from New Orleans but I grew up in North Carolina"

If ever I felt like I didn't belong in North Carolina, those days had nothing on the isolation and awkwardness I experienced in Lafayette. It was hard to believe that in the same year that Cash Money Records had taken over for the '99 and 2000's, Lafayette was a city stuck in time and racially segregated. The year we moved there, they'd finally decided to integrate the all Black school on the North side of the train tracks, Northside High, with the mostly white students on the South side that attended Lafayette High.

This integration changed everything. The veteran students of Lafayette High were ready to march and protest for their rights of individuality being taken away at the arrival of the new students and a new school uniform mandate. Inexplicably the uniforms were implemented to "ensure the safety of the school" and to show that all students were now Lafayette High students. Everyone questioned why it was not an issue before. What was so dangerous about the Northside High students, that safety could only be guaranteed with an LHS-emblemed green shirt and khaki pants? Even in the North Carolina schools, we didn't wear uniforms, so I felt their pain. However, I also lived life in plaid uniforms while attending a NOLA public, majority Black, elementary school. Was this yet another place where "Black" equated to "unsafe" and uniforms represented law, order, and suppression of individuality?

Tensions were high from day one of ninth grade. Everyone assumed I was from the Northside because of my skin color. Soon everyone figured out I wasn't from 'round there at all. I was too educated and well-spoken for the Northside High crew, and too poor and ghetto-adjacent for the Lafayette High students.

I joined the track and field team in hopes of earning a coveted Varsity Letterman jacket, the ultimate symbol of belonging, but I didn't fit in with the athletes either. The athletes were right, I was just a two-year visitor to the track team. I quit right after I thrust my arms into the sleeves of that Letterman jacket. In search of community, I tried to befriend the other kids from my Honors and AP classes, but compared to my early street smarts, they were a bit too sheltered and naïve to form real connections outside of the classroom.

While my older sister, The Professor, was still a student at Lafayette High, I was welcomed into her friendship circle. But then they left in the Spring of 2002 after graduation. I was alone and experiencing a teenage existential crisis most days. I struggled through high school wondering who I was and if I'd ever settle in at this miserable place. Lunch was the worst time of day to be a loner in a school divided. I carried my tray away from the register and stared at the sea of seated students. Where do I sit? I didn't belong with anyone.

To avoid the whole scenario, I often hid in the bathroom or skipped lunch all together and stayed in the library. My mom helped me escape this bleak reality and sometimes picked me up and took me to lunch at Popeye's or Raising Canes. She knew it was a hard time for me and wanted to help in the little ways she could. She was determined to make sure her girls would not have to endure the adversities she faced as a teen. She became my very own stay-at-home Super Mom, chauffeuring me to and from school, attending every track meet and awards ceremony, cooking all my favorite meals from back home, and taking on the role of Thelma to my Louise as we conspired daily about how to sneak me out of the single unguarded exit at lunch time.

Of course, I couldn't expect my mom to break me out of that hellish place every day, so I needed a Plan B. Luckily, I discovered my favorite teacher, Mrs. Castille, had an Art class during lunch, and she allowed me to attend that class instead of going to lunch. She was one of only a few Black teachers at the school. She understood my struggles and helped navigate a series of events: when I was denied access to gifted classes due to my out-of-state evaluation, punished with in-school suspension after being falsely accused of skipping class, excluded from homecoming court because of a very specific quota of three minorities, and when I was singled out by a racist teacher who wanted me to agree that Tommie Smith's "raising his Black Power fist" at the 1968 Olympics was a horrendous act of defiance and treason. Instead of harboring hate and nursing discontent for everyone, Mrs. Castille allowed me to vent but encouraged me to channel my energy into positive areas. She showed me that I was a capable visual artist, a prolific poet, and a musical theater enthusiast! Who knew? She introduced me to Aida, CATS, and Rent which are some of my fondest memories of that time.

Mrs. Castille was an amazing Black female educator. She saved my life. And I eventually made a friend, Shandrea, who gently coerced me out of hiding and remained a guiding light in my life for over twenty years. I am forever grateful to have met my best friend, but I will always stress the absolute necessity and importance of having teachers like Mrs. Castille that look like their students, who can relate to them in a way that is both reassuring and uplifting, and who can help them channel and navigate the darkness into positive areas.

In the three-and-a-half years I attended Lafayette High, I faced numerous obstacles and challenges that made me question if life was even worth living as an awkward Black girl that didn't fit in anywhere. But God! But my Mama! But my art teacher, Mrs. Castille! They gave me the strength and guidance to carry on, to have the courage to be myself in a lonely sea, and to have the persistence to keep running the race even when the finish line kept being moved a few feet further beyond my reach.

HBCU (HISTORICALLY BLACK COLLEGES AND UNIVERSITIES) BLUES— LETTING GO OF PERFECTIONISM

In the Summer of 2004, I enrolled at Xavier University of Louisiana with a full academic scholarship. I went to college in hopes of becoming an Oncologist. Like so many Black women before her, my aunt had died of metastatic breast cancer. In the span of three months, I watched her decline from her usual quick-witted, mess-starting, hyper-active, dramatic self to a thin, withered, empty shell of the person I knew and loved.

My sister convinced me that attending college with her was my pathway to freedom. I figured I'd better choose a major that would afford me the opportunity to really make a difference and earn a living wage that would provide a measure of freedom I had yet to experience. I proudly told anyone who inquired, "I'm a Biology Pre-Med student at Xavier University." The rigorous curriculum and high expectations of the staff in the Pre-Med office reminded me all too often that maintaining straight A's was a lot easier in high school than college. I worked my ass off to earn a 3.45 GPA my Junior year, a damn near impossible feat after surviving Hurricane Katrina and being displaced to Fayetteville State University in 2005.

That catastrophic natural disaster was a traumatic, world-shattering event and not surprisingly, many of my peers didn't return to Xavier. I returned, stuck it out, and persevered through what was the longest uninterrupted academic year of my life. We had no summer break to make up for the time lost from August to December. The grinding year impacted my mental health, and my grades suffered. I earned two Cs for the first time in my college career! I felt like my life was over and my hopes and dreams were dashed. It didn't help that the director of the Pre-Med office met with me to discuss my chances of getting into medical school at the start of the next school year.

"Sorry kid. You got a C in Anatomy and a C in Biochemistry. You didn't pass the MCAT. God's honest truth is, you ain't getting into nobody's Medical school," he delivered the news flat and straight.

I left his office in a blur. The familiar feeling of chest-tightening, heart racing, light-headedness indicated the onset of a panic attack. I called my mom crying, frantically trying to convince her I was seconds away from death. Her rapid-fire questions and calm tone forced me to recount the entire tale. She expertly used her motherly magic to restore gravity to my world that had begun to float away. Feet firmly planted back on Earth, I continued to wonder: All I had worked for my entire life up to that point, now gone because of two C's?

That was my last time going to that office. Three years wasted. Turns out, a 3.45 GPA wasn't good enough to go to Medical School or to keep my academic scholarship, which required a 3.5 GPA for juniors and seniors. As much as I wanted to give up, I had too many credits to change majors. Knowing my background and personal motivations for attending Xavier, my college advisor encouraged me to apply for a competitive Fellowship Program that focused on Cancer Research at Tulane University. I applied with fifty other students and to my surprise and delight, I was selected along with a group of three young women. Take that, PreMed office!

My victory celebration was short-lived. In the thick of it, I realized that this work was not a suitable career for me. Who knew the world of Cancer Research was so incredibly boring and cut-throat. I ambled down the freezing cold hallways, barely awake, with my timer in hand ready to notify me when cell growth had finally occurred. Drudging along, I'd hear stories of co-workers being sabotaged. Cells were contaminated, phones were allegedly bugged, and there was the constant mad dash to get published and present your scholarly research before someone else stole your hard-earned work.

As graduation approached, I decided it was best to take a year off and figure out my next steps. I reached a pivotal moment in life where I knew I would have to let go of the picture-perfect image of the life and career I thought a bachelor's degree would secure. I was lost, but I knew my family would help me find the right path.

RUNAWAY TEACHER—A JACK OF ALL TRADES

I was adrift after graduation and was looking to my family to help me navigate my next steps. Yet, one reassuring aspect of being a full-fledged adult meant I was ready to settle down. Right. I mean isn't that the next step in the order of events to adulthood? In my gap year post-college graduation, I explored the possibility of living with my high school sweetheart, Bama, and we were thinking of marriage. We lived together for three months before we both acknowledged that we weren't meant to be. He had too many family obligations and it was clear they didn't like me. I would never be accepted by them. In the end, he chose his family, and I chose myself. I still didn't know what I was going to do with the rest of my life, but settling for an unhappy marriage was not on my to-do list. It is one of the best decisions I have ever made.

The Professor urged me to return to New Orleans in 2009. I always knew my big sister would be a teacher and a leader someday. She persuaded me to be her teacher's assistant, paid bi-weekly out of her own salary. I don't know how she did it. There were so many kids all needing so much help and remediation. Most days I didn't eat lunch but instead went to my car to take a brief nap and recharge my battery. The work was hard, draining, but rewarding. I was too busy to lament the failed relationship.

Motivated by a short stint as a teacher's assistant, I found myself back at Xavier University working in the Biology Tutoring Center. It was there that I delved deeper into helping struggling learners and was encouraged to earn my Master of Arts in Teaching while working full time as the Biology Tutoring Coordinator. I worked towards my second undergraduate degree in between daytime tutoring sessions and attended classes all night from five to nine pm. Trying to find a delicate balance between working full time, attending night classes, and student teaching was my introduction to the busy life that lay ahead of me.

My first year of teaching began in the Fall of 2012, and I taught high school Biology.

"Bayyy-bay, I don't think you know whatchu doin'."

Sharell lobbed this insult at me. She was a spirited eighteen-year-old in advanced AP Bio. The whole class sucked in their breath, looked at me, and waited for my response.

I paused. Then burst out laughing!

And the whole class followed suit.

The scene was so familiar. There I was, back in New Orleans with a room full of teenagers, who were just a few years younger than me, who had brutally honest, spitfire personalities just like the family members I grew up with in Bigmama's house! What the hell had I gotten myself into? Whatever it was, it felt like home.

My first five years of teaching were rough. Most nights I'd go home and cry over stacks of books and incomplete lesson plans. I lost thirty pounds from the stress and anxiety of never feeling prepared and failure to care for my basic necessities like food and sleep. My social life was non-existent and romantic relationships didn't stand a chance. I ended each year feeling like a complete failure and resigned from one school to try out another. I was not exaggerating when I told my family and friends I was sick and tired of teaching. But what else was out there?

By 2018, I realized I was growing, evolving, and ready for something new and different. I was passionate about teaching and a strong advocate for my students. However, the job of teaching proved to be not just time consuming, but life consuming no matter where I went. I'd been to six schools in six years. Every year a new group of kids tugged at my heart strings and elicited all the love and attention of biological children. Yet, the local education system proved to be broken beyond repair. I constantly felt like I was trying to stop a massive hemorrhage with a thin Band-Aid. I knew if I didn't take a step back, I would be swallowed up in despair. I decided to try something new. I was sure life would get easier if I made the choice to scale down and work part-time as a teacher, while simultaneously trying out a trendy part-time job as a "gig-worker." Both decisions ended in tragedy.

The 2018-2019 school year was the worst of my life. Working part time came with all the same stressors and burdens of full-time teaching without any of the benefits. I had no health insurance and battled a range of illnesses all year. These were dark times, and I held eleven jobs just to pay my bills. I left one job at two o'clock pm and went to another at three. On Thursdays, my off day, I picked up shifts wherever I could, ranging from background acting to parking lot flagging.

On weekends I maxed out my gig hours. I did every odd job available, from unarmed security, to brand ambassador, to buffet attendant. I swallowed my pride and did whatever was required for me to stand on my own two feet, refusing to return home and transfer yet another financial burden to my family. My Super Mom, The Professor and Red Ant, Bigmama, and her descendants had given this Mother Owl wings. I promised myself from then on, I would use them to fly!

AUTONOMY
...the ability to make your own decisions and act independently, without being controlled or forced by others; Self-governance; Freedom

I look in the mirror some days and still can't believe that I'm almost forty years old. Where did the time go? Wasn't it just a few years ago when I was a teenager walking the streets of Downtown New Orleans during Mardi Gras? Only a few months ago when I was hopping on shuttle buses to the club and bumming rides with strangers to make it back to my college dorm room before the two o'clock curfew? Didn't I just buy my Camaro to celebrate my independence and my thirtieth birthday? It seems like just yesterday when I quit my tenth teaching job and booked a solo cruise to the Bahamas the following week!

For some on the outside looking in, it may appear that I am still unsettled and lost. After all, I am still single, no kids, and now working at the twelfth school in thirteen years. But I know those are external measures of success. I am a survivor! I climbed my way from rock bottom to the solid foundation you see today, and I am immensely proud to have done it.

I am a brilliantly curious young woman that was so nurtured by her family that she never had to experience what it felt like to be unwanted or unloved. I am a compulsive perfectionist who doesn't know how to settle for mediocrity. My mentors and the women that went before me broke glass ceilings and swept away the debris so my path was cleared. I am a gentle, kind-hearted soul that would give her last dollar to help someone in need. I am an optimist who knows, as well as J.R.R. Tolkien, that "Not all who wander are lost." In fact, wandering has been the cornerstone to leading a fulfilling, autonomous life; operating on my own terms, exploring what makes me feel happy and whole. I don't answer to anyone, don't have to explain anything, and will only be unapologetically me!

While I may not know what's next for me, I rest assured in God's promise that "Eye has not seen, nor ear heard, Nor have entered into the heart of man, The things which God has prepared for those who love him" (1 Cor 2:9). I love the Lord, and I know great things are on the horizon.

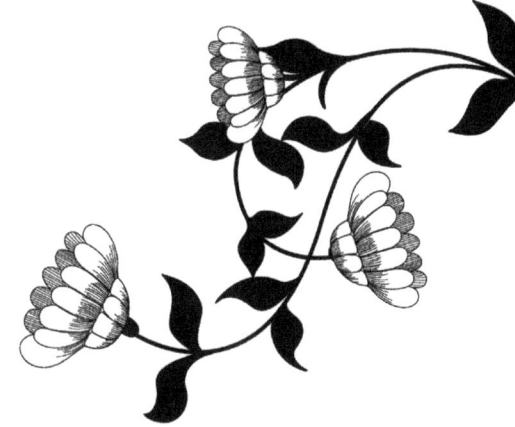

Introduction to
DOMINIQUE LUSTER

Dominique Luster is a one-part archivist, a one-part researcher, and a full-part natural-haired bourbon connoisseur turned entrepreneur. As an archivist, she has worked in the cultural heritage and memory fields for over ten years and has become known as a champion of Black history and Black-centered storytelling. After working at universities, libraries, and museums across the country, she understood that history is not merely a listing of events in chronological order. But rather, a meticulously curated phenomenon of power. All too often, the stories of marginalized communities are suppressed, oppressed, erased, or forgotten. With this as a north star, Dominique started her archival consulting firm, The Luster Company, as an outpouring of spirit to help organizations uplift, honor, and tell stories that represent the lived experiences of the Black diaspora.

In Relentless Pursuit of
LEGACY

BY
DOMINIQUE LUSTER

THE SCRIPT FOR MY TALK WAS METICULOUSLY WRITTEN. Then rewritten and rewritten again. I rehearsed it ten times a day for the past month and did live practice sessions twice a week. There was nothing more to be done. The moment was here.

I was invited to talk about my work as an archivist. I'd spent the few years before working in and with Black communities to help preserve their history through the archive of a mid-twentieth-century photographer named Charles "Teenie" Haris. I'm extraordinarily grateful for this work and the communities I've worked with.

Archivists preserve the original letters, photographs, documents, diaries, and other primary source material created by people, organizations, and governments. As far back as early human civilizations 5,000 years ago, someone was responsible for documenting the world around them: the grain that was traded, the kings that ruled, the gods that were worshiped, and the famines that people survived. The early scribe kept the record and helped establish the history. As the scribe became the knowledge keeper, the place where that knowledge was stored became the archive. And over hundreds of years, the archivist has continued this tradition and preserves history as it is being made.

Depending on whom you ask, the history-making process is straightforward. When an event occurs, a person records their experience in either writing, photography, art, music, dance, oral tradition, or a plethora of methods. This event is then corroborated by another person's accounting of the event. Even if their experiences differ, they are often confirming the existence of a person, place, or thing. The record created by the original person(s) is socialized, and other independent entities further authenticate or deny the validity of the event.

An example of this history-making principle is the event of a person's birth. In many cases across the world, when a person is born, the event of their birth and acknowledgment of their existence is documented by a parent in some fashion. That event is then co-signed by a hospital, for example, which creates its own paperwork authenticating the existence of the person's birth. Then, the child's birth might be socialized by making calls and sharing photos, during which independent entities such as friends and family members create their own proof (i.e., the capturing of their own photos) and further validate the event. Down the line, the hospital's birth record might be used as third-party evidence of a person's birth for identification or passport purposes. One hundred years from now, even if the person is no longer with us, the person's existence is considered a fact because of the overwhelming amount of evidence, and the history-making loop continues.

However, many events or occurrences are not so clearly delineated. The existence of chattel slavery in the United States is so highly corroborated that its existence as a period in history is considered a fact. Yet, the day-to-day lives and experiences of enslaved individuals during the period of chattel slavery are highly contested and considered debatable. This is primarily because those holding power over enslaved individuals largely created the documentation from that period. With limited opportunity to create a first-person account of their lived experience, the story of the enslaved person was systematically suppressed.

However, history is not everything from now backward. That is the past. Historian A.J.P. Taylor argues that "history is not just a catalog of events put in the right order." For years, I have asserted that history, the *story* of what happened, is a series of strategically curated choices that can uplift some or erase others based on the decisions of those who maintain the power to curate it. Whether we realize it or not, history is decided, chosen, and specifically designed. Some events and people are included. Most are not. Moreover, what is included is hardly ever chosen or described by the people who create it. These choices are made by the history stewards (and gatekeepers)—people like archivists.

Because of their role in the history-making process, archives are often presumed in a distinguished position as "truth"; people tend to implicitly trust the evidence found in primary sources, such as original letters and photographs. We view them as the closest thing to being there because, in many ways, they are. Yet, this is one of the most critical oversights of modern society.

Archives are not neutral; they are selected.

The selection of certain objects to be included in the "archive" over others is an assertion of power, and these decisions affect the evidence we can look to and thus our understanding of our history. As a society, our cultural philosophy is profoundly impacted by what we believe about ourselves—but do we ever question the fullness that shapes those beliefs? Is history truly written by the victor? Or is the victor's story merely the version that was selected to be included in the archive? And even more, what does this mean for marginalized, colonized, or ethnically-minority communities?

On this scheduled day in the summer of 2018, as a young Black woman archivist, I had thirteen minutes to explain this incredibly complex concept and discuss how marginalized communities are impacted by archival practices to a sold-out audience of over 800 people.

I stood in the wings backstage and peeked out from behind the curtain.

Nope! Don't do that. Bad idea.

I turned away from the curtain and leveled my eyes at the back of the stage. I over-corrected my posture and stood tall in my sequined black heels. I held my head high and lengthened my spine into a power pose. Power posing was first suggested in 2010 by Dana R. Carney, Amy Cuddy, and Andy Yap. I understood that there was not enough clinical evidence to prove whether power posing actually works. Nonetheless, I posed my heart out—it worked for me! I centered myself with eyes closed, hands on my hips, and a prayer whispered on my lips.

The emcee called my name. I opened my eyes, exhaled

doubts, inhaled confidence, and strode onto the stage and into blinding lights. The raucous noise of the crowd seemed muffled, it echoed just beyond my hearing. I stood by the tall TEDx letters and gave the talk that changed my career. Too bad I don't remember a single word I said!

But I do remember where it all started.

In 2012, I came home to the University of Kentucky from a summer of studying abroad in Berlin on a Fulbright program. I was entering my junior year of college, and like many of the nearly twenty-percent of Kentuckians who lived below the poverty line, things were financially strained for me and my family. One thing led to another, and months passed when I couldn't pay my rent. I was evicted from my apartment at the end of the fall semester.

At the time, I was in the undergraduate theater department, studying lighting design and technology. I was a straight-A student who'd worked hard throughout her first few years and was granted increasingly greater privileges in theater. By junior year, I was invited to solo design the lighting for the winter dance concert, which was typically reserved for seniors; it was a significant opportunity.

In the theatrical world, there is an in-depth rehearsal where all the technical components, such as lights, sets, and props, are meticulously matched with the action on stage. This is called a tech rehearsal. Until this point, the dancers are in the studio practicing away, the set pieces are in the shop being constructed, and the lights are being hung by technicians according to the lighting designer's vision. This special rehearsal is the first moment in the lifecycle of theatrical production in which the various components of any show begin to come together as a holistic piece of art.

When I was evicted at the end of the fall semester, I moved home which was an hour away from campus. Tech rehearsals often last a few days, and without a place to stay, no money for a hotel, and only an old, limping vehicle, I didn't get to the critical tech rehearsal for the winter dance concert I was designing.

Like I presume of many young people, I felt isolated in our financial struggle. I grew up with the old church adage, "If God don't do it, then it just won't get done!" I believed then, as I do now, that the Lord will always provide a way. However, at that time, I didn't understand the community aspects of the gospels so well, and I didn't reach out to friends or family to ask for help. Instead, I hid at home.

There are moments in life when one's path is resolutely changed. Moments that are a distinct *before* and *after*. Missing that tech rehearsal was the wrong choice. I don't need hindsight to tell me that. I knew it then that I was leaving people hanging and that there would be consequences. But at the time, I also didn't have the skills to figure it out. However, I have great compassion for the young lady whose path was resolutely changed and who was about to become the main character in her own story.

When the spring semester started up, I still had no housing for the semester, so I drove back and forth one hour each way to class. On the first day of lighting-class, the professor who was forced to cover for me in the tech rehearsal asked me to stay after class.

"I'll give you one chance to explain," he asked, desperately staring at me for anything that might make a shred of sense.

Still too ashamed, I refused to confide the truth.

"There was a problem, but I've solved it," I lied.

He continued to stare, shocked by my response. I don't blame him; I would be too.

In consequence, I was removed from the winter concert and all previously assigned lighting roles. I went from a rising star to repairing old light fixtures in the shop. All my work up to that point was negated with a single failure. To this day, I hold his words solemnly in my heart: "It only takes one *hell naw* to ruin a thousand *attaboys*."

While I knew he was right, and I knew I was done in the lighting department, I also knew that my drive from Louisville to Lexington was an hour each way. Regardless of who was right or wrong, I had to drive home after that defeating conversation and back the next morning. It was the spring semester of my junior year, and my chances of getting a recommendation to a graduate theater program seemingly disappeared. I had to pivot. But first, I had to find a place to live.

I stayed on my friend Katie's couch, living out of a suitcase for a couple of weeks. Her roommates started complaining, so it was back to the hour-long commute and hoping the car wouldn't crap out each way.

At the same time, I was in an academic fellowship for humanities undergraduate scholars. The Gaines Fellowship in the Humanities is a competitive two-year program designed to nurture students to pursue their interest in public issues and facilitate a nuanced understanding of the human condition through the humanities.

The University of Kentucky had over 4,500 juniors my year, and only twelve were accepted into the Fellowship. The cohorts and the program's staff become exceptionally close within the academically demanding environment. After a few weeks of my unsettled housing situation, I confided in the executive assistant of the Fellowship program, Connie, whom I considered an *auntie*. I unequivocally believe in the power of the Auntie. Sometimes, this is a woman who is related to you. Sometimes, it's your friend's mom. Sometimes, it's a lady at church. Regardless of how she comes, the Auntie is part of your village. She encourages, she advises, she tells you when that boy is no good and the best Aunties offer cookies and snacks with their desperately needed bits of wisdom.

I sat across from Connie's desk, taking a little too much advantage of the candy bowl. I told her about my housing situation and the fallout in the theater department. In her wisdom, she knew that a prolonged housing issue was a critical junction in my life's story; my path would worsen dramatically without resolution.

She mentioned my situation to the Executive Director

of the program, who was a member of the Presbyterian Church located on the edge of campus. The church owned neighboring properties, including a sizeable three-story house primarily used for youth group social events. They also used the first floor as a men's shelter twice a month. And the attic level was converted into a one-bedroom apartment for people in need.

The church offered to let me rent the upstairs apartment for $600 for the semester. See! I knew the Lord would provide!

I moved in the same evening they made the offer. It was already dark outside when I trudged up the creaky stairs with a backpack, a blue suitcase, and a thin air mattress. Alone, I opened the apartment door directly to a bedroom space with wooden floors and yellow lights. I set the suitcase down and unpacked my scant belongings. Nowhere to put away my clothes—I stacked them neatly on the floor. It did not take long to inflate the air mattress and fit the sheets onto it. I brought one blanket but realized when I made the bed that I had forgotten a pillow.

The attic apartment teetered atop the imposing property. The high ceilings and dark wooden floors shrunk my already meager belongings, and I felt small. The tall, uncovered windows peered out into a black night and rattled loudly with the wind. I scrambled between the sheets and pulled the blanket into a knot under my chin.

Everything I had been emotionally carrying from the moment I left my previous place flooded my mind. The eviction that wasn't my fault. The missed tech rehearsal that was. The endless hours in that limping car. The constant feeling of being overwhelmed. Tears slid sideways over my face and pooled onto my pillow-less bedding. I repeated prayers until I eventually fell asleep.

I woke the following day with a slight lingering sense of fear but a larger sense of accepting my reality. A poem I learned as a kid in the Whitney M. Young Scholar program came to me all of a sudden:

I can, I must, I will be somebody.
In all that I do, spirit tried and true
Only the best of me will come shining through.
Not my mother, not my father, nor my enemies who try to stray me.
But by my own undying heart, which beats on ever steady.
It is with this pledge that I set my life
And with it I vow to be
A winner first. A winner last.
For everyone to see.

I was alone. I was scared. I had no money. But I had a roof over my head, smarts in my brain, and ability in my body. I can do hard things. I will be somebody. I was made by God for such a time as this.

That morning, I fully explored the empty apartment. The bathroom shared a wall with the kitchen. I found the light switch, and when I flicked on the light in the bathroom, I found my roommates. Thousands of roaches scattered across the floor and fled beneath the walls and under the shower. It was like a dark floor that aggressively shook itself loose to reveal the light, gray-colored floor beneath it. Another thing to solve.

Over the next days and weeks, we tackled the infestation. One thing down. The amazing church staff dropped off a bed, a round kitchen table, and a few dishes and cookware. Another problem solved. There was no individual heating unit to the upstairs apartment so, so I swiped a space heater from home, pulled together a little furniture, and brought over more clothes. It was coming together. Now I needed to attack the next hurdle and get a job.

The university library was hiring and were paying $15 an hour, which might as well have been millions and was an answered prayer. I was a straight-A student, a Fulbright scholar, a Gaines Fellow, and there were loads of other things vying for my attention. My twenty-year-old-self debated Socrates in by day, and attended governor's balls in gorgeous gowns by night, all while hiding housing insecurity, financial distress, and an unsure future. I smiled and I waved, and I was tired. A cushy library job checking out books seemed like the perfect opportunity to catch my breath. Although I was anxious and unsure about the interview, the library hired me, and I was earning money. Another problem solved.

It is hard to remember how I did it all, but the library became a sanctuary. It was the perfect job for me, but it was not checking out books. It was an experimental, grant-funded program called Learning Lab. It was designed to expose academically diverse undergraduate students to the world of archives, by pairing them with collections based on their interests and introducing them to archival skills.

Given the nature of library work, it is common for education, history, or English majors to enter the archival field. But what about pre-med students, or architecture students, or theater majors like me? Without programs like this, I would have never known where the archives were on campus, much less be exposed to the field of archival work. I'd come to find out that there was a world of specializations within archival work that fits just about everyone or any interest.

The manager was an archivist. Staci was bold and beautiful and was only the second Black woman teacher-figure I'd ever had in my life. The first was my High School orchestra teacher Ms. Tamika, who was also bold and beautiful.

I was briefly introduced to using original archival documents while working on my thesis, but the library job was my first experience learning what it meant work in an archive. We started with reading old handwriting. Then moved to physically rearranging a folder of letters from the eighteenth century. Then I worked on a Playbill collection which combined my theater knowledge with the newly developed archival skills.

One day, Staci introduced me to the first archival collection related to African American history I would ever work on. It was a Minstrel show posters collection. In all my years working in theater, nor my entire lifetime as a young

Black girl growing up in Kentucky, had I ever learned about the complex history of black-face theater in this country.

In working on that first collection, I came to understand that people tend to overlook the power of the archivist. A person who determines which documents find a final resting place within the shelves and which do not is a remarkable role. Only the tiniest amount of material created by humans actually makes its way to an archive. It is staggering how the first-person evidence of people, places, events, traditions, or ideas of Black life and culture get lost to modern generations because it was not deemed important enough by the archivist at the time.

That first collection, led to the next, and the next. Before I knew it, I looked up and found myself on a TEDx stage five years later talking about the power of archives.

From that day to this, I feel profoundly called to preserve Black history. I don't remember any of that meticulously written TEDx script—only five years after working on that Minstrel poster collection.

I rehearsed the talk ten times a day; I delivered live practice sessions endlessly. And yet, flash forward to that day, the moment on that stage, I only remember standing there in a pair of sparkly black heels recalling the chaotic season of my life when God resolutely directed my path.

I forget what I said, but I remember Staci. And Holly. And Steven. And Andrea. And Lae'l. And every other archivist who taught me the words I shared with the world from the stage that day.

The audience cheered as I walked off stage, and gratitude flowed through my body and leaked out of my eyes. I was grateful for every opportunity, for every change of direction. And I thank those long dark windows, the buffeting wind, and the scattering roaches because without them, I would not see how far I had come.

Because I am somebody, and the best of me is shining through.

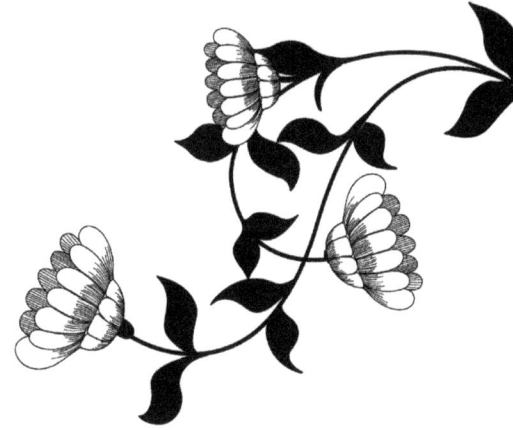

Introduction to
EBONY ALLEN

Ebony Allen, LCSW-BACS, is the Founder and Director of Brook Haven Counseling and Consulting Services. Her community-based practice reduces the stigma of mental healthcare in marginalized communities through therapy, education, and consulting. With nearly two decades of experience, Ebony is a trusted leader in adolescent and family care, creating safe, inclusive spaces for healing and growth.

A proud New Orleans native, Ebony earned a bachelor's degree in psychology from Northwestern State University and a master's in social work from Southern University at New Orleans. She is clinically trained in trauma-informed crisis response, school-based interventions, and bio-psycho-social assessments. She also holds multiple professional certifications, including the Qualified School Social Worker designation from the Louisiana Department of Education.

Throughout her career, Ebony has served as a juvenile probation officer, middle school disciplinarian, and hospital-based therapist. She founded a nonprofit to empower Black girls and young women in New Orleans. Ebony also served on the Institutional Review Board (IRB) for the Institute of Women and Ethnic Studies, where she evaluated proposed studies to assess potential risks of harm and ensure they had no negative impact on underrepresented communities.

Ebony is an adjunct professor, teaching courses on diversity, equity, and inclusion, and holds an adjunct committee seat with the Louisiana State Board of Social Work Examiners. Her professional accomplishments include being inducted into the National Honor Society of Social Work, and she was a featured speaker at the 2025 NASW (National Association of Social Workers) Conference.

When not working, Ebony enjoys being a loving wife and mother to two beautiful girls. Along with crafting, cooking, and listening to music, she embraces her creative outlets to find peace and joy.

In Relentless Pursuit of
PEACE

BY
EBONY ALLEN

THERE I WAS, STANDING OVER MY MOTHER'S LIFELESS BODY. My throat burned, my mouth filled with water, and I remember my stomach tightening as bile tried to push its way up.

She was still.

Time stopped as she lay on the hard gray kitchen floor tiles. My hearing was muffled and my vision narrowed. Everything paused and the energy in the room drummed as loud as a New Orleans second-line band.

My thoughts raced.

Was she scared? Did she experience pain? What the hell happened!?

With the quiet, following those initial moments of confusion, an intense sense of peace settled within me. Even before it was announced, I knew she was gone. And even before the officer on duty confirmed it, I understood there were no indications of foul play.

Of "natural causes" at the young age of fifty-eight, alone in her home, my mother left me. The examiner confirmed her death at 7:00 pm. By 7:05, the examiner mumbled condolences, packed up her materials, and slipped out of the little apartment.

Frozen. Shocked.

My feet in concrete and my limbs stiff, externally still, internally reeling, I am not sure how long I stood like this, it felt like hours, but was probably just a few minutes.

As the evening light began to fade beneath the kitchen blinds, Iceola, my mom's mom, swooped in. I've always admired her, but that day solidified her hero status for me. I'm convinced I saw a Black woman's superhero cape flutter in behind her. Instead of joining my confusion and shock, she swiftly moved into action. After all, things needed to be done.

"Ebony," her calm but stern voice regrounded me, "Bring me some towels and a blanket."

I was still frozen. So, JQ, my husband, obeyed her order to collect the requested items. I fought back tears as heavy as boulders as I watched his arm extend the things she needed.

With quiet strength and grace, she took the cloth and kneeled next to mom. Her movements were smooth, comforting, and each stroke was filled with the love we were all accustomed to. In her final act of service to her daughter, she peacefully covered mom's body as we stood there together in silent solidarity.

After five years of reflecting on those moments, I realize my grandmother's behavior wasn't simply resilience. It was instinct. It was expectation and understanding. She knew what must be done and was showing me that no matter how painful the moment, you hold it together and keep moving.

There are many lessons I learned over the years from Iceola Ellzey. But on January 7, 2020, she taught me the power of the Unicorn Effect—the circumstance of not acting from a place of pain, fear, or even confusion, but simply getting shit done.

Iceola exemplifies what it means to be a Black woman. How, even in our deepest grief, we push forward.

This quiet endurance, this unspoken rule of strength, is passed down for generations. My grandmother learned it from her mother, and my mother from hers. I saw it in my aunts and cousins. I see it in the countless Black women I encounter throughout my career.

It is the same resilience Dr. Briscoe writes about—the phenomenon of Black women carrying the weight of the world, not because they should, but because they have been conditioned to believe they must.

That day with my mother and grandmother was a stark reminder of the resilience I was indoctrinated into. Growing up on the Westbank of New Orleans, I witnessed my aunts raising their children as single mothers. They juggled work, life, and love, all with their strength defying the weight they carried. My best friend Teshawn, a teen mom, navigated her undergraduate nursing program and then triumphed in graduate school with a stubborn determination that refused to let her circumstances define her.

In my professional encounters, I saw countless Black women fight through barriers, climbing into leadership with grit and grace. These women, like my grandmother on that day, showed me that resilience isn't just about getting by—it's about thriving, no matter the odds, Their strength has fortified me and shaped how I face my own challenges, guiding me through my life.

The thread of their resilience is woven into the fabric of my own journey and ever-changing story. From my earliest memories to the hurdles I've faced throughout my career, their lessons are a centering force. An anchor. And so begins my story of the constant subconscious battle of Upending the Unicorn Effect.

When I consider Dr. Briscoe's research and definition of The Unicorn Effect, I admit that it's taken some time for me to see the Unicorn in myself. Sure, I'm constantly moving and shaking. I'm juggling work, family, and entrepreneurship. I'm attempting to build my professional career by working twice as hard for half the opportunities and accolades as my white and male counterparts. I'm trying to show up in the best way possible for my friends. I'm code-switching. I'm teaching. I'm mothering. I'm consulting. I'm cooking. I'm eating healthy. I'm volunteering. I'm attending church. And while it's true that I love my family, friends, and career, it is also true that I'm tired. But that's just what we're supposed to do. Right?

The idea that a Black woman's strength is proven through her ability to withstand the pressures of life while not asking for much in return is outdated, unhealthy, and dangerous. Nevertheless, we've adapted the multi-generational trope of *the strong Black woman*. As a therapist specializing in the mental health of Black women, I support my clients' journey in shifting from a mindset of *strong Black woman* to one where they are whole and free. I help them explore the idea that strength and happiness should not be at the cost of their peace, rest, or joy.

My mom, Ms. Pam as most people called her, fought many battles throughout her life.

My siblings and I witnessed the ones she couldn't hide, but I know there must've been a mountain of struggles we didn't see. I wish she'd known that she was a Unicorn even when she didn't have to be.

Unfortunately, I don't always take my own advice; then I spend unnecessary time beating myself up. Oh the irony! On my journey, I've powered through. I still battle imposter syndrome wondering if my degrees, certifications and experience are sufficient to take a seat at the table. I pray that in those moments, God continues to remind me that even without those credentials, I am enough. I pray for the strength to continue creating my own seats and when necessary my own tables.

There's no prize at the finish line for the sacrifice of managing it all. The true prize is the joy we experience through unapologetically pursuing peace.

The road to finding peace is littered with potholes and distractions. Some lessons are learned the hard way and blocking out the noise of other people's demands and expectations is critical. Focusing on peace sets the tone for my life.

Three common elements afford me the endurance to step into my fullness. Areas of intention are unique to each person, but for me, *friendship*, *gratitude*, and *boundaries* influence my arrival into a place of peace.

FRIENDSHIP/CONNECTION

My husband, JQ, and I are connected. It goes without saying, our relationship is my air. Our connection was molded and is sustained through divine intervention. Just as the connection to my natural family, God chose us for each other. He put us together and decided we would love and support one another.

Although I've been with my husband since I was a teenager, my focus here is friendship. Friendships have a power that cannot be overstated: the beautiful connections with others that we, in our sound mind and body, select. I find joy in publicly verbalizing my love and affection for my girlfriends. Anyone who's witnessed our bond throughout the years, truly understands why they deserve it.

During early adulthood, I experienced a friendship breakup that gutted me. Dismissing the march of red-flags in that relationship almost dismantled the self-esteem I'd worked so hard to build. I swore then, and still stand by the conviction, that it will never happen again.

JQ, whom I was dating at the time, invited me to dinner. My girlfriend Rickie joined us at one of our favorite seafood restaurants. What started as a fun night with friends ended with the worst and yet silliest argument I've had in my life. JQ and I ordered Diet Cokes. Rickie commented that the whole idea of Diet Coke is stupid, and that people should either just get Coke or avoid sodas altogether. I responded that I didn't mind the taste of Diet Coke and that some people, like JQ, used it as a tool to step down from sugar.

Rickie went on a tirade that ranged from how much I had changed to how I didn't know-it-all. Her rant of insults continued with a litany of grievances that she clearly was prepared to hurl at me. They rolled off her tongue so much with ease that she must have rehearsed them. None of them were accusations or statements of something I had done to hurt or betray her. Instead, they were things she believed were true of me and of what the pecking order of our friendship should be. She thought I was too loud, my personality was too big, and I should "stay in my lane."

Rickie was usually demure. She used a small voice and presented herself in the most pristine manner. Her appearance meant everything to her.

During this conversation, which was really a monologue, she made sure I knew I wasn't as pretty as she and I wasn't smarter than her either. She said I should remain a tomboy and give up ever trying to do my hair and master make-up skills, which wasn't my first priority and not a great skill I possessed.

I was starting my new life. I had a man who loved me and I was on track to be the first one in my family with a college degree. I was in a great space. But through her words, what I heard was that I was an ugly, ghetto girl and that I should stay that way. Whew!

Bewildered, JQ and I left the restaurant, and I was devastated. The ride home was quiet and tense. I'm not sure what she was thinking. I've never asked what he thought but during that long ride, I returned to being a broken, dark-skinned little girl with no self-esteem or confidence. That was the removal of the first brick of that friendship which would eventually lead to its destruction. I spent weeks wrestling with those feelings. I fought hard to remind myself of my worth and value.

In fairness, Rickie and I were barely out of childhood. Neither of us could have predicted the lasting effect our words could have on others. But those words have stuck with me. I'll never forget how that conversation made me feel. India Arie once said, "There's a blessing in every lesson." Well, I'm glad that I knew her at all.

Rickie's temporary presence in my life left a lasting impression. Even though the friendship didn't last, the impact did—and for that, I'm grateful. There's an old saying that people come into your life for a reason or a season. I didn't see it then, but time has made me deeply grateful for the lessons buried in my friendship with Rickie. What I once saw as betrayal, I now understand as necessary growth. That relationship taught me how easily love and loyalty are confused with control and competition—and how vital it is to choose myself, even when it hurts.

Today, I have close girlfriends and relationships. If something comes up, we address concerns directly in the moment. We show up and root for each other. We laugh, cry, and pray together. For the past two decades, my girlfriends have mourned each of my losses and loudly celebrated my wins, even the small ones that felt insignificant to me. They nudge me when I move outside of the steps of God. And as if that weren't enough, they always compliment my make-up, which I've finally mastered!

Without judgment, competition, or jealousy, they

provide a peaceful article of armor that adds to my strength. I've healed from the trauma of past sour friendships. My hope is that, as a fellow Black woman who is a unicorn in her own right, Rickie has found success, sisterhood, and any other factors necessary for her peace.

GRATITUDE

Being grateful for your possessions, both material and not, was a staple lesson within my community while growing up. None of us had much. But what we did have, the elders taught us to give thanks for. At twenty-eight years old, the concept wasn't new to me. I understood it, but I remember the moment when I realized poverty was behind me.

My six-year-old daughter, Ja, was going to perform a dance at a school assembly. I started the morning as usual by whipping up breakfast, setting out the kids' clothes, and attempting to get them ready.

Dress—check. Vest—check. Shoes and knee-high-sparkly-rainbow socks—oh no! no socks! Okay, new plan. I'd drop the kids off at school and run to JCPenney to get knee-high-sparkly-rainbow socks for Ja's assembly performance.

Leaving the house that day was more chaotic than usual. Ja, was in full meltdown mode because of the socks. Jay, the four-year-old, was planted firmly by the door, arms crossed, explaining in detail why she was not going to school today. We couldn't find Ja's left shoe and someone, probably Jay, let the dog out. Whoosah!

Somehow, in the middle of all that noise and drama,

we made it out the door. As we turned the corner and approached the school, we said our morning prayer and settled into our routine. I dropped off the girls and hustled to JCPenney.

The girls' section had black, white, and pink socks. Nope, not good enough. I searched while the clock ticked in my head and my heart pounded with nerves. Then, on a hook near the bows and mini purses, I spied knee-high-sparkly-rainbow socks! What luck! I was relieved. They were adorable with lots of glitter and shine. These were exactly what Ja wanted. Great. I'd grab them, then race to school so she would have them before the assembly.

Beep beep went the register as the cashier said calmly, "That will be twenty-five dollars and thirty-seven cents."

"Excuse me?"

"That will be twenty-five dollars and thirty-seven cents, ma'am," she repeated, looking up at me.

"Did you ring them up twice?"

"Um, no," she peered at the blue letters on the screen.

"Is that the right barcode?" My brow knitted together, trying to understand how one pair of socks could be twenty-five dollars.

"Yup," she smiled "It looks right."

The line behind me was growing and I could sense the frustration from the other shoppers.

Should I get plain white or black socks? Would the pink socks be good enough?

No, that wouldn't do. The costume called for

knee-high-sparkly-rainbow socks and if I came with any less Ja would be crushed. I swiped my card and headed for the door.

My steps faltered as I approached the exit. I stood still, took a deep breath and with my big exhale came a flood of unexpected warm tears. Trying to breathe and collect myself, I stood there for quite a few moments, crying and trying to compose myself, my vision swam as I watched the lady who had been behind me pass with annoyance and a brief shake of her head.

I just bought twenty-five-dollar socks!

Suddenly, the memory of a nine-year-old me and a missed McDonald's trip crowded to the front of my brain. The Victory Baptist Church Youth Group was going to McDonald's after service, and I begged my mom to allow me to go.

"Only if I can send you with food stamps," she yelled out the front door.

The group leader overheard her and offered to pay for my food. All the kids also heard the answer. In hindsight, their parents were probably getting food stamps too, but I didn't think of that. At that age it wouldn't have mattered. I was crushed with embarrassment. I made up an excuse about not feeling well and didn't go.

My childhood was peppered with similar experiences. We couldn't get anything *extra*. I leaned on family members and the community to help me attain specific things. My mother was a single parent with just enough resources to provide basic needs. She did not have the ability or the desire to get anything more. If I wanted or would have needed sparkly, glitter socks, we would have had to borrow the money, wait for a family member to help out, or go without.

Standing at the JCPenney exit I remembered those experiences. The rush of gratitude was punctuated with the gush of tears. It hit me—I now have the freedom to choose how I spend my money, instead of being forced to do without. My children will have choices and experiences I did not have.

There will be no McDonald's food stamp stories for my babies. I was in a place to provide not only their basic needs but also their wants—even if what they wanted was twenty-five-dollar knee-high-sparkly-rainbow socks!

BOUNDARIES

As therapists, we offer insight, treatment and guidance to help clients maintain boundaries when necessary. Often, we know what to do. We teach it. However, we do not always model it.

Sometimes the realization that you are not holding a boundary smacks you in the face.

On a Friday before a big and complicated workshop I was hosting over the weekend. My to-do list was on life support, and it wasn't even noon yet. I had back-to-back client sessions scheduled, a stack of emails, a meeting to confirm details for the workshop, and somewhere in the midst of it all, I was supposed to eat, sleep, and maybe breathe.

My phone rang. It was Kay, a girlfriend I know and love

and someone who's always been there for me. As always, I stopped what I was doing to be her rock, her safe space, and her emotional landing pad. Because that's what I do, right? I fix things. I help. I show up, even when I do not have it in me.

I answered with a sinking feeling and prepared to receive her burden. As the conversation progressed, her words weighed me down and tension crept into my shoulders. Kay was overwhelmed and life was hard. She needed advice, reassurance, and encouragement. I listened, nodded, and hummed small words of affirmation.

I was happy to support Kay. But, inside, something was shifting. I was exhausted, not just physically but emotionally. I had nothing left to give, yet here I was, stretching myself thinner and thinner, pouring from a cup that had been empty for weeks.

The next day I suffered a stroke. Yes, like a literal stroke.

The hospital was a scary Twilight Zone. I still dream about the blaring lights, weird smell and incessant tones emanating from the machines. I was poked, prodded, and tested for hours and then days. The doctors discovered that my stroke was caused by a patent foramen ovale (PFO), an undetected hole in my heart. My cardiologist says it's been there since birth, but I never knew. I had no symptoms and had always been relatively healthy. Still, the combination of the PFO, my weight, and constant stress turned out to be a dangerous mix. While I'm grateful to finally have a documented cause for the stroke, I often use dark humor to point out that the hole in my heart came from losing my mother.

The turn in my health was a giant red flag reminder to take my own advice and set boundaries. My stroke and related health issues weren't anyone else's fault. They had no idea of the internal battles I was fighting. It wasn't their responsibility to know or be cautious. It was mine. Yet, in the depths of grieving the loss of my mother, grandfather, and pre-pandemic life, my relentless drive to be everything for everyone left me dangerously depleted.

The stroke forced me to confront the fact that my inability to set boundaries put me in physical, emotional, and spiritual harm. In the quiet space of recovery, I recognized that I needed help beyond medication and rest. I needed the very thing I had dedicated my life to providing to others—therapy.

I started working with a Black therapist who helped me unravel the heavy layers of grief and anxiety. I committed to entering the therapeutic space differently than I had before. I removed my clinical hat and became a client. I was open-minded. I was curious and thoughtful.

She helped me see through the self-imposed pressure to show up, even when running on fumes. I was reminded that setting boundaries isn't about pushing people away, it's about preserving my energy, honoring my needs, and protecting my heart. Literally.

I discovered that the Unicorn Effect was not a mark of resilience but a recipe for burnout. With every session, I further understood that saying no isn't a rejection of those I care about, but a necessary act of self-respect and self-care. Now, I do what I can when I can, choosing not to overcommit or give in to the unrealistic pressures of perfection. I still struggle with anxiety, finding myself fixated on fears about my health, my kids, and life in general. However, setting boundaries has become one of my key coping skills. I practice protecting my mental and emotional space. I want no part in anything that doesn't speak life or add to my peace. That part of me is still a work in progress, but by setting those limits, I manage the anxiety and find peace by focusing on the things I can control.

UNICORN EFFECT

The Unicorn Effect isn't an ugly monster. The idea itself isn't the enemy. Having the ability to juggle as many things as you'd like and do them all well, is an actual gift. It is one of the amazing characteristics I love about being a Black woman. We are magic. But upending the idea of the Unicorn Effect is about refusing to be drained dry to maintain an illusion of strength. It is unnecessary and unhealthy to love others in a way that sacrifices ourselves.

The story of my mom's passing always briefly paralyzes me. Not just because we lost her, but because it was so immediate and unexpected. I often wonder how things might have been if her tomorrow had come. What plans she might have had, what words she would have shared. Losing my mom taught me to value every single moment. Drawing strength from my resilient grandmother and even the hard lessons of a lost friendship, I've learned that true friendship, gratitude, and clear boundaries are the keys for me to find and live in peace. These pillars are grounding truths on my journey toward fulfillment.

Every day, I hope to honor the legacy of those who came before me by living boldly and authentically, setting a powerful example for my daughters, nieces, and every Black woman I encounter. I want them to know that while they can achieve anything they desire, they also deserve to live a life of fullness and inner peace without compromise.

Cherish your life, nurture genuine connections, and stand firm on your boundaries. I urge you, amid being your own version of an ethereal Unicorn, to bravely and unapologetically pursue your peace!

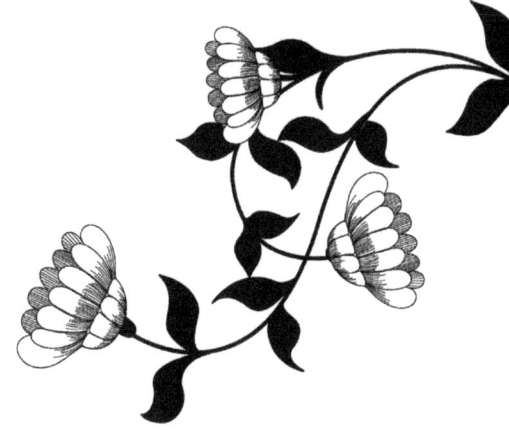

Introduction to
JAWAN BROWN ALEXANDER

Dr. Jawan Brown Alexander, originally from New Orleans, leverages her diverse experience as an educator, executive, community advocate, non-profit leader, entrepreneur, and leadership coach. As the CEO of Maroon, Inc., her mission is to foster leadership in underserved communities nationwide.

Dr. Alexander has partnered with governmental bodies, educational agencies, small business leaders, and nonprofit organizations to enhance strategic initiatives that engage and empower underrepresented communities. Through her efforts, she has helped build essential relationships that strengthen civic infrastructure.

Jawan has supported education-based organizations in realizing their potential and demonstrating measurable growth. As a trainer and leadership coach, she also designs tailored professional learning opportunities for educators, nonprofit leaders, community leaders, and civic leaders. Recognizing the significance of research in leadership across business, civic, and educational sectors, she co-founded a mentorship program in 2020 aimed at BIPOC (Black, Indigenous, and People of Color) leaders pursuing their terminal doctoral degrees in leadership, focusing on research in leadership, education, and community while implementing best practices.

Jawan has participated as a guest speaker, moderator, and panelist at both local and national conferences. Under her guidance, Maroon hosted events such as The New Orleans Freedom Riders Town Hall and a discussion with the CEO of the Trayvon Martin Foundation. Additionally, Dr. Alexander has appeared on educational podcasts and radio shows related to small businesses' growth and educational support in marginalized communities, and her written work has been featured in various local and national publications. She holds both a master's and doctoral degree in leadership and is a proud alum of Southern University and Xavier University. A lifelong learner, Dr. Alexander has studied at Harvard's Leadership Institute, is a member of the Louisiana Superintendent's Academy, and is Goldman Sachs' 10,000 Small Businesses Alum.

In Relentless Pursuit of
PURPOSE

BY
JAWAN BROWN ALEXANDER

THE ROUND TABLE
A unicorn is unique. Is one of a kind. A unicorn is strong, has rare power, and is hidden away.

My story is one that reminds young women that we are all unique and that through life's journey, God may have tucked his little unicorns away, but he is doing it to build you, fortify you, and protect you for your calling—your assignment. I was recently listening to a B. Simone podcast, and Jason Wilson, the featured guest—a mentor, author, and inspirational leader—said, "Things that are precious are hidden away for safekeeping."

As little girls, our strength is built up and stored away, and it shows up when we are adults and empowers us as we mature. As we run this marathon called life, it is important for each of us to unpack our Genesis story. It helps us to understand our journey—one without judgment and with the measure of grace we deserve.

As a little girl I always felt that I was different than those around me. I wasn't lonely, but I was siloed. God hid me away, getting me ready for an assignment that I was not yet privy to. Somehow, I understood that even with my isolation I'd someday fully exercise my gifts. I saw the framework of what my future looked like, only the details were not yet fully visible. I was determined at a young age and influenced by three important women in my life.

MY THREE OVERSEERS
I envisioned the three of them sitting at an ornate round oak table.

They sat comfortably in plush leather chairs and discussed my inquisitive nature. This little girl, who would be hilariously unfiltered, would blossom and grow into a young leader with attention to detail and a quest for wisdom and ultimate purpose. Each woman agreed to their roles and nodded confidently understanding this was the right path and strategy for the little unicorn.

Wyne, my mother, was the enforcer—the bad cop, the stern one who promised to get the little one in line. Bernice and Mary, my grandmothers, were the good cops. They agreed to build me up and hold me accountable when needed. They wisely selected others to bring into the fold—Brenda, Lil Mary, Sharon, Dionne, and Alice to name a few, and they pledged to stay true to their assignment.

They all recognized leadership qualities in me. Each of these wise women pushed me to lead. My grandmothers were my best friends growing up, and as I matured into womanhood, my mother became one of my closest confidants. Wyne, Bernice, and Mary recruited other women along the way, and I recruited my own tam too. They were my life coaches before that was even a thing.

WYNE

At an event last year, the Mayor's spokesperson talked about my father's stewardship but highlighted my mother as the one leading from the wings. In the 70's and 80's she took young Black children to play tennis and other sports that were not being offered in our communities.

My mother was a strong, stoic, behind-the-scenes leader who shifted her positional power and used it to prop up and cultivate other leaders. Lady, as her grandkids call her, is a beautiful woman, with dark skin and high cheekbones. Because of the dark hue of her skin tone, her family gave her a nickname that was common to folks with darker complexions. I am not sure if she fully embraced the name, and I often wondered if the name was ever triggering for her. During my teenage years, although my mother and I had a complex relationship, I always admired her beauty, her poise, her sense of humor, her infectious laugh, and her ability to be direct when other people turned away from bigger family and community issues.

My mother poured so much into me, my sister, and my brother. I grew up with my younger sister, Jade—and my little brother, John, came along a lot later. John and I are thirteen years apart and even now I feel like I am his second mother.

My momma was a guiding force and someone that I looked to as a model of what a beautiful dark skinned Black woman could be. She was the epitome of style and grace. She was a fashionista before the term became popular and when she entered a room, everyone noticed.

Her personality and smile pulled people in, and her direct approach was undeniably authentic. As a kid, I often listened to her talk on the phone after work and her laugh made me laugh too. Her gorgeous white teeth lit up the room when people commented on her beauty.

THE GROWN-UP TABLE

My mother noticed at a young age that I processed information differently from my peers. The things that I appreciated were not what people my age generally admired. I was different. As a little girl, I admired my female teachers for their strength and intelligence. During my elementary school years, I realized that I felt older and more mature socially than the girls in my friend group. I remember as a little kid listening to my parent's albums and CDs—playing R&B music all through the house on some Friday nights and Saturday mornings—Luther Vandros and Anita Baker—which is what my parents listened to and not as much of the pop music that kids my age liked. This adventurous spirit extended to food too, I tried foods that most kids didn't like.

I was inquisitive, interested in how the world worked, and wondered if I would receive the answers to my internal questions—as I came to terms with being built differently in terms of how I viewed the world, my environment, and my community. I was called an old soul, and I knew as a little kid that I possessed a wisdom that I could not really explain.

Why are you always inside with the old people? My younger cousins and little sister would often ask. I sat with the older women in the kitchen as though I was invited. If you were ever looking for me at a family gathering, I was more than likely in the presence of older women while all the other kids were playing or watching TV.

I loved being in the presence of my female relatives—the stories, the wisdom, and the realness. Often, I was instructed to leave the room when conversations got too spicy, but until then, I soaked it all in and relished my seat at the table.

Holidays were filled with plenty of food, music, and laughs. One Thanksgiving holiday, at my grandmother Mary's house, the women were hustling back and forth—from the kitchen to the living room carrying food and finishing up the meal—turkey, dressing, ham, mac-n-cheese and all of the other things that we couldn't wait to consume. As the women spoke in a harmonious cadence, I followed them room to room. Mary realized I was trailing behind her and sent me to play with the kids so she could finish the story she was telling the others.

On the way home my momma reminded me to be a child as long as I possibly could and try not to grow up too fast. Momma knew that I was different, she recognized my inquisitive nature and that I was surrounded by these dynamic females that I looked up to, but she also wanted to make sure I didn't skip my youth and innocence.

I was drawn to Mary and Bernice. Their lives were fascinating and the way that they showed up as matriarchs was inspiring. They were both strong yet caring—Bernice gave us the biggest hugs every weekend when we arrived at her home, or the way Mary would pick me up from school if I had majorette practice or wasn't feeling well. These were old-school grandmothers who were a part of the village, helping to raise us up.

My grandmother Bernice's two-bedroom, one-bath house on Mistletoe in Hollygrove in the heart of Carrollton, was a place where love lived. Big kisses from a woman who admitted that she lived for her grandchildren and prayed for us constantly. Bernice was an amazing cook who took care of her baby brother after her mom died when Bernice was a young mother. She was a housekeeper who worked for a wealthy white family. Through that connection and through her church, Bernice traveled the world and told me all about her long journeys to France and parts of Africa.

Bernice, or Tille as she was affectionately called, was a woman who was a devout Methodist and leader of the usher board. Born in the early-1900's, she donned a white usher uniform each Sunday.

Mary Roussell, my dad's mom, was the younger of the two and became a mother when she was sixteen. Mary lived with my grandfather Willie in a double shotgun house on Valence directly across the street from where the Nevel Brothers grew up. Mary's house was always filled with music and the soulful smell of Creole cuisine. Mawmaw, which was the name her grandchildren gave her, was a housewife and entrepreneur who was into fashion and home decor, and spent hours in the kitchen cooking incredible meals for us. Her home was lively, often with music playing, and the smell of good food filling the house from the front door to the back.

These two women were my refuge, and they taught me a lot through their examples. My quiet nature came from Bernice, but my ability to have fun and speak boldly came from Mary.

BUILDING THE LITTLE UNICORN

What I knew at an early age was that God wanted me to rely more on my wisdom than my smarts. He gifted me with women—my mother, grandmother, aunts, and older cousins that I looked to as mentors. Older relatives were my heroes. Like my old pastor says all the time, "Everything you need is already in the house." I didn't have to look outside of my family and extended family for role models.

Leadership Lessons

Sometimes people are blessed to encounter one unicorn but, in my family, the elders were raising up all courageous young women. Strong women with the ability to lead, share their real stories of triumph, sorrow, and heartache. Women who would pray their children to success and point them in the right direction. Women who were not afraid of the backlash; they knew what they were doing and saying made sense.

My first leadership lesson came at Woolworth's Department Store. Woolworth's was a smaller version of today's big box stores. When I was six years old, my mother was in the store shopping, and my little sister and I played in-between the racks of clothes. Wyne told us to stop horsing around.

Like nearly any child that age we continued swinging through the clothes as though we hadn't heard her instruction. The spanking was delivered with a stern conversation about how I knew better. She emphasized that I was the oldest, I was the leader, and I knew better than to behave that way.

THE SHIFT

With all her beauty, authenticity, and essence on full display, abruptly her most impactful superpower would be tested. My mother's strength was challenged when faced with an overwhelming personal loss.

One day after school, my sister and I were in the living room watching The Price is Right. I was about to do my homework when the phone rang. I watched my mom's face tense with worry, and I knew something must have been wrong. My grandfather was in an accident. She gathered us up and we were hustled out the door. Her rapid movements revealed her fear and anxiety.

My grandfather passed away in an unexpected tragedy. My momma still had that gorgeous smile, but she wasn't showing it as much. This was the first time I remember seeing her broken—the woman who was leading our family was bruised. During this time, I felt my mother's heartbreak. Abruptly after the funeral, my grandmother Bernice came to live with us for a few months. Initially I thought this was more about my mom keeping an eye on Tillie Momma but now I realize my grandmother was keeping an eye on her little girl. My mom was her youngest and Tillie's motherly instincts kicked in.

I was seven when this all happened. By that next year, I had my eighth birthday, and my mom recognized that because I was socially advanced, she needed to be sterner. At the time, I attributed it to her loss and that because of it our relationship shifted; but looking back, my momma was preparing her little girl for the real world. At that age, I was sensitive to her correction because it was so direct, and my young mind was not able to understand that she was getting me ready for life.

Through my teenage years and into my late twenties, I struggled with understanding the right moves to make. I didn't quite understand what to do with my natural abilities, and I needed direction. I understood the what but not the how. The women in my village were there to nudge me, correct me, and remind me of my calling.

THE SEEDS

I used my experiences to choose my mentors and life coaches. Women that I saw characteristics and traits that Wyne, Mary, and Bernice shared. I took everything that I learned from them and used compassion and wisdom to push me to my purpose. As I grew up, my cousin Dionne was my first role model outside of my mother, aunts, and grandmothers that wasn't adult. D was just old enough to mentor me without trying. It was more about her actions and her leading by example. Dionne has always had an even temperament. Although I made connections with young people my age, I enjoyed creating bonds with women that shared their life stories and wisdom with me. Those relationships intrigued me.

Now at fifty, I have two women in their seventies who are in my circle, one friend who recently turned sixty, and a family member who is approaching sixty. Evidently my desire to sit with wise women has not changed. It allows me to tap into my gifts in a bigger way. I am not afraid to have someone challenge my thinking in a productive way. From my Grandmother Mary to my Aunt Brenda, Mary Johnson, to Alice, to Leila, to Mardele, to my Grandmother Bernice, to Wyne, to my Aunt Sharon, to Diane, to Linda, to my Aunt Sandra, and my Aunt Pam, to Aurelia, Sharon Paul, Gina, Michelle, and Dionne they gave me strength and confidence. Many of these women are still with me today and I still confide in them as my journey continues to unfold. Even the elders who have transitioned, their words and deeds stay with me and have shaped me as a leader.

Each member of my circle took turns connecting the puzzle pieces for me—a young woman who at times felt lost and confused about what my calling and leadership journey would end up being. Dr. Rene Akbar, one of my professors at Xavier University, asked a key question in a doctoral class: *Are leaders born or cultivated?* For me, it was both. I am a hybrid. Leadership is a gift, but also God had to place the right courageous, smart women in my life to cultivate my gifts.

MY ASSIGNMENT: NEW ORLEANS

In 2006, I moved back home from Chicago with my husband and son, I thought about my work in education and leadership differently. Up to that point, I worked in the central office as an administrator from starting as a clerk at the early age of nineteen. Stepping back onto New Orleans soil my aspirations and my commitment were tied to the community. My leadership journey was about community action and community impact. I set community-wide leadership as my purpose; my potential and my promise was connected to the city of New Orleans. The city that my mother and grandmothers called home.

Six years before Hurricane Katrina, my boss and mentor, Leila Eames, asked when I was planning to finish my undergraduate degree. I put it off to start my family, but she wasn't having any of that and said that I was too smart not to get my degree. So, eight years after starting my collegiate journey, with so many personal responsibilities, I finished my degree! I then joined the School Leadership Center's cohort, where a long-time educator, Debra Moran Reimonenq, mentored me.

Having started my educational journey, I marched on and got my master's degree. For the first time, I knew all the lessons were coming together both personally and professionally. Things were starting to make sense.

Dr. Armand Devezin, the man who hired me as a clerk at the school district's central office, said that he saw leadership in me and told me to go into the schools and work there. I was destined to work directly with the community, children, and educators to understand what they were experiencing. The central office was a representation of my comfort zone, and I couldn't see myself leaving.

My parents were both long-term educators and I leaned into my observed experience. I watched them at the high school where they taught. I saw what it meant to be an educator. John, my dad, climbed the ranks and became a school administrator, and Wyne was a teacher and led the dance, cheer, and majorette teams. I admired their ability to lead. They were committed to the kids in our community, and little did I know, they had gifted me with a blueprint to follow.

THE WORLD THEY PREPARED ME FOR

These experiences propelled me into my work as a leader, and the shadows of my inner circle have shaped who I am now as a leader. As a forward-thinker, I often think without boundaries, I take risks, and I don't allow people to be distractions. My three heroes provided something different: they knew when to speak their minds, they knew when to be direct and when to be discreet, when to wear a poker face, and when to be courageous. These were the lessons that I needed.

Staring down a life-changing illness at the age of sixty-six, I sat down with Mary on the porch outside of her home and she explained what her last wishes were going to be. What strength it must have taken to be so introspective and realize that she was going to transition soon. Having a conversation this deep with her eldest granddaughter had to be difficult for her but she didn't show emotion, only a courageousness that is unexplainable.

I took the strength that I saw that day and realized that I needed to be vulnerable after Mary's death. But I didn't really allow myself the grace to grieve because I saw so much strength around me. I understand now that I did not fully acknowledge Mary's death until six years later. Being courageous is important but you cannot stifle your sadness. Allow grief to naturally flow while being brave in the moment.

These lessons have propelled me through the ups and downs of professional and community leadership. Whether it was the opportunities that I had as a young woman who had to stand up to a high-ranking official who wanted to reprimand me in front of an entire room of my colleagues. Or when I worked as a leadership coach, my white female supervisor asked me to go with her to lunch on my second day at work, and she said to me, "We don't work that hard around here." She was speaking to me—a young woman who only knew how to work hard to improve things! Through the lens of my elders' wisdom, I understand that there is a double standard. It is amplified by the world showing you that you are, in some cases, seen as an outsider.

Think about ambitious women. This double standard is often directed at them. Men are seen in personal and professional spaces as hungry and confident, while women are demeaned and called thirsty and bitchy. Women's ideas are borrowed and used while the woman is placed on a shelf and pulled down to admire when it is convenient for the world to be fascinated by all that we have to offer.

Wyne told me during our car rides: this world doesn't

owe you a thing. That was her way of preparing me for how some people in the world might unfairly view me, look to take advantage of my gifts and turn away when it was time to recognize my impact.

Kamala Harris, our former Vice President, has a story that is a microcosm of what we have seen since the pandemic. Black women were used as a *shield* to save the world, especially after the brutal death of George Floyd.

When we look at New Orleans for example, there was a female Mayor, interim police chief, sheriff, and Superintendent of Schools placed in leadership positions or elected. All these women are women of color. All of them have been publicly scrutinized in ways that we have not seen happen to their male predecessors. Male counterparts are protected in ways that women do not receive the benefit of. Why?

We color outside of the lines. We are directly speaking to and handling issues in a way that removes the cover and shines a light on stuff that the world is not ready to expose. So, when the world looks to come down hard on a Black woman, it is about shifting and removing her influence.

My Three Matriarchs along with many other amazing women in my life were building me up long before I understood. They were my foundation. I know that as I continue to embrace the memories of both of my grandmothers, they are cheering me on from heaven. I continue to relish my mother's fiery spirit; although she has slowed down her fire still burns.

I am now charged with helping develop our next young women leaders and more experienced professional women. I realize that I owe my spiritual fortitude, my moxy, and my ability to keep my focus on what's important to my three heroes and all of the other women in my circle. The women in my matriarchal circle (my "m" circle) modeled how I needed to use my voice in a way that is sometimes calm, sometimes poised, and sometimes relentless—but always fearless. This is the gift that keeps on giving and the legacy that has extended across generations.

The Three Matriarchs who sat at that broad oak table were there for their family, experienced great losses, and made huge sacrifices so that their descendants would accomplish more than they ever imagined.

Sometimes people are blessed to encounter one unicorn but, in my family, the elders were raising up courageous young women. Strong women with the ability to lead, share their real stories of triumph, sorrow, and heartache. Women who would pray their children to success and point them in the right direction. Women who were not afraid of the backlash when they knew what they were doing and saying made sense.

Through their individual and collective stories, Wyne, Tillie, and Mary show us all that a Black woman's most important job is to commit to planning for, showing up for, and guiding the little Black and brown unicorns in their charge. I carry the power of these women in every space that I enter. Now, we have been called to raise *our* families, improve *our* communities, and shape *our* world into a place where we all have a seat at the large oak table.

> *"The higher purpose of my life is not the song and dance or the acclaim, but to rise up, to pull up others and leave the world…a better place." — Viola Davi*

We are unstoppable.

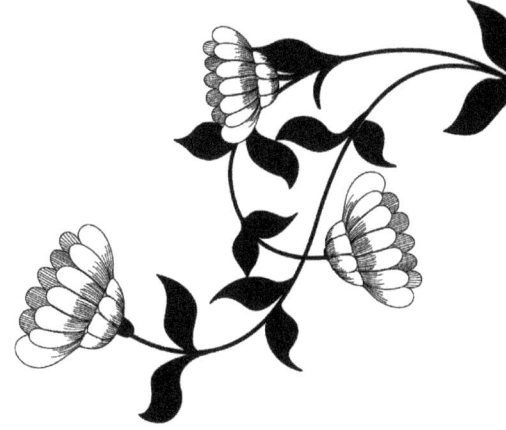

Introduction to
CHANISE REESE-QUEEN

Dr. Chanise Reese-Queen has over twenty years of experience in professional development, education, and training within diverse academic, nonprofit, and healthcare settings. Her career has focused on directing and managing continuing education and volunteer leadership programs, facilitating strategic initiatives, spearheading conferences and events, and leading staff and teams across multiple sectors.

Committed to lifelong learning, Dr. Reese-Queen holds a doctorate in educational leadership and management, a master's degree in public and community health, and a bachelor's degree in human relations. She is currently pursuing a Master of Science in Law with a focus on healthcare law. Chanise has also earned certifications and completed specialized training in leadership, learning design, technology, and mediation.

Dr. Reese-Queen's leadership experience includes serving as president of a regional continuing medical education alliance, a board member for a national professional education organization, and a senior leader in continuing medical education at a prominent academic medical center. She is dedicated to fostering learning opportunities, promoting diversity, equity, and inclusion, and leveraging technology to enhance educational accessibility and effectiveness.

Passionate about empowering others, Dr. Reese-Queen enjoys helping women discover their infinite potential while embracing their authentic selves. Through her signature workshop, *Own Your Awesomeness*, she inspires women to advocate for themselves and confidently own their accomplishments.

Dr. Reese-Queen is a Zumba instructor who enjoys working out, running, and staying active. She is an avid reader who loves spending quality time with her husband, family, and friends.

In Relentless Pursuit of
INFINITE POTENTIAL

BY
CHANISE REESE-QUEEN

IT STARTS WITH FAMILY.

When I reflect on all the things that have shaped my life, it starts with family. I grew up in a two-parent household. Both my parents worked hard, making sure my brother and I were cared for. They didn't just ensure we had what we needed; they exposed us to more—fine dining experiences, travel, the kind of living that made me see life as something to explore.

My mom shopped at boutique clothing stores and dressed me up in cute outfits. And she threw me a birthday party every year—up until I was six, when my brother was born. After that, the birthday parties shifted to celebrating us. Every single year, there was a full-blown celebration for us both. Now, when I look at the pictures from those parties, in every photo, we were surrounded by parents, grandparents, aunts, uncles, and cousins.

Even surrounded by family, I wasn't the little girl playing with doll babies or dreaming of a Barbie mansion. That wasn't me. While others were styling their dollhouses or collecting all the latest Barbie outfits, I was roller skating and biking. I loved games like Operation and Twister—games that made you think and got you moving. The only thing close to a doll I had was one of those styling heads where you could braid and curl the hair. It was a white doll head because that's what was available.

I didn't fit into those traditional female roles. And as I got older, that theme stayed consistent. Societal expectations tell us "Grow up, get married, and have kids. Raise your family." Young women raised in the church get extra pressure to have this life—get married, have kids, raise a family. That plan didn't resonate with me. Sure, I thought about getting married at some point, but not in the fantasy-driven, big white wedding kind of way. And kids? Honestly, it wasn't something I thought much about.

SCHOOLING

School? I've done it all. I went to two Historically Black Colleges and Universities (HBCU), a women's college, a for-profit university, then a state university. I like learning. I like the challenge. But I wasn't the traditional student. I worked two jobs while going to school—days, nights, weekends. I paid my own tuition. I commuted instead of living on campus.

Those were my early years—the straight-out-of-high-school years. I started at one HBCU for two years, transferred to another for three more years, and still didn't graduate. Five and a half years of school, no degree. Instead of finishing school I got engaged.

I was focused on getting married and I was working and making good money. Finishing school just wasn't the priority. Life has a way of circling back. The jobs I applied for all required a degree, and I still hadn't gotten that important piece of paper.

Every May, when graduation season hit, I felt it. That heavy weight of expectation. That constant, nagging reminder that I did not graduate. Hearing *Pomp and*

Circumstance crushed me. Every single time. It was like the universe reminding me—You didn't finish. You didn't graduate. You didn't cross that stage.

I felt that for fifteen years. The feeling of unfinished business. Until I decided, on my terms, to go back and finish. I earned my undergraduate degree and that first important piece of paper. Then I kept going.

I pushed forward and got my master's degree, took a two-year break, and tackled my doctorate. Another pause and then went back for another master's degree—scheduled to finish in May 2026. Yeah, I've been in school forever. But you know what? I did it on my terms, in my timeline, and I did it because I love learning.

The educational journey wasn't just about degrees. It was about finishing. We start things all the time, and sometimes, we don't finish. There is powerful meaning, confidence and joy in finishing something started. If you're in school and never finished, go back! My husband, Derald, always says that one of the greatest words in the dictionary is *finish*.

If you've never started school or a trade, and that is a goal for you, then start and finish. It doesn't have to be a traditional four-year college—get a trade, a certification, a skill. Learn something. Derald says, "The more you learn, the more you earn." And let me tell you it is true!

Invest in yourself. As women, especially as Black women, we constantly pour into others. We support, we uplift, we handle everything for everyone else—and we put ourselves last. That must stop. We must invest in ourselves. Take the time. Make the effort. Prioritize you.

While in school, there were nights when I caught a flight, came home, and typed a ten-page paper before sunrise. I got a B. No AI. No shortcuts. I always went after the A. I wanted that 4.0. I pushed myself to be excellent in everything. I did in school from junior high through my doctorate. I strived for As.

And now, I'm in school for my second master's degree, and to be honest, I don't care about the A. All I care about is passing. That's it. Sometimes I get a seventy or lower on a quiz or test, and I shrug it off like, I have nothing to prove. The A doesn't get me more money or more learning—it's just another measure, another expectation thrust on us. It doesn't make us better, or even smarter, people.

I'm getting this second master's degree because I love learning. How refreshing would it be to be able to learn without this assessment? It is part of the process for now. If I pass, I'm good. No stress, no pressure. I'm learning, and that is what matters.

LIVING

My mom, Annie, loved to party and celebrate hence the big birthday bashes. Even while she loved to celebrate, she was serious when it came to academics and success. Annie pushed me the hardest. She knew that I could always do better, be better, and she made sure I knew that.

This drive and intensity led to competition becoming

my way of life—academics, work, everything. I thrived on it. I wanted to win. I worked hard in school, and I was valedictorian in ninth grade and made the honor society in high school.

Annie was one-of-a-kind. She spoke her mind, said what she had to say, and didn't care who didn't like it. I loved that about her. Her strength and confidence allowed me to embrace my own power. She showed love through hugs, kisses, corrections, and celebration. Even then, she would admonish me, "Nisey, you can be so cold at times." She wasn't wrong. I'm not the most emotive person. I never have been. I am direct and analytical.

It doesn't always make sense to me when or why people cry. There are all these expectations to *feel* things. In church, people questioned why I didn't feel the Holy Spirit. Um, I don't feel anything, except maybe hungry and looking forward to dinner afterward. Although mom questioned it, she accepted my stoicism, and that allowed me to accept myself. I know that everyone experiences things differently.

In the middle of getting my doctorate and working full time, my mom died of pancreatic cancer. Like everything, she battled the disease, and the family fought alongside her. My husband, Derald was on dialysis, I had recently started a new job, and I did not have a lot of time-off available. Derald and I had recently moved into a new home, and we were just getting settled. Hustling to and from work, school, my parent's house, and hospice was exhausting. And I did it all while keeping a strong face for Mom. Often my days ended in tears in the tub, the warm water doing little to sooth my soul or ease the pain.

I went into oldest daughter mode. People were depending on me and looking to me for strength. I had decisions to make, a family to lead. People came to me with questions and expectations. But I wasn't alone. I had my dad and my brother—we clung together, and we fought her disease together. Her being sick created a sadness with weight, a heaviness to bear. We all felt it and took turns with the weight, carrying the burden. Everyone in the family pulled together to battle the disease. Dad stayed by her side, ensuring mom took her medicines and fixing her food. Terry did his part, always showing up, talking with her, and keeping her spirits up. Mom and Terry spent so much time joking and kidding around—you always hear their laughter.

Even with the family fighting together, some days I wanted to walk away from everything, just disappear, just give up. But society expects us to keep moving. Keep your chin up! You got this! You can do it! That's all bullshit. Why can't we give ourselves grace, why are we not allowed to grieve?

We all, but particularly as Black women, must know when enough is enough. It was okay for me to call my advisor and say "My mom passed. I'm taking a semester off." It was okay to tell my supervisor about her passing and she responded by telling me to "take as much time as you need."

Y'all, it's okay not to have that *I'm Every Woman* complex! *"I'm every woman, I ain't braggin' cause I'm the one! You just ask me, ooh, and it shall be done."* Chaka Khan shared the burden women carry to be everything to everyone and to get everything handled.

Hold up. Shall be done? For whom? By whom? Because I know you're not talking about me! As a Black woman, I realize I don't have to carry and do everything. I don't have to push through at the expense of myself. We have to learn to take a damn break!

Losing my mom was a defining moment for me. We spend so much time trying not to die that we forget to focus on how to live. That moment made me ask myself: What am I doing to live? I don't want to just survive. I don't want to just exist. I want to thrive and live life to the fullest.

The family bonded together to beat the disease, but the cancer won in the end. Mom's passing broke my heart and pierced my emotive shell. Even now, losing her stings, and tears slip down my face as I type. She was so much to me, loved me so much, and I can barely tolerate the ache in my chest.

LIVING SINGLE

My parents loved each other, and my dad took care of his family. I remember Dad picking up a second job to make sure our family had everything we needed. He didn't just work hard—he made sure everyone got where they needed to be. Every morning, Dad drove me and mom to work. He dropped me off, then Mom, even though our jobs weren't on the same route. He passed his job, doubled back to drop us off, and then finally headed to work himself. And, at the end of the day, he came right back, picked me up, picked Mom up, and then we headed home.

If my mom was still alive, they would have been married for fifty-seven years. Like any married couple, my parents had their ups and downs. But they showed me what a great marriage was—love, some challenges, and then more love on top of that. Their relationship shaped my life and my identity. Accepting something less than their example for a marriage is something I would never do.

My brother, Terry, is one of the kindest, smartest, most caring people I know. He married before I did. And when he was dating his now wife, Darnnell, he cared. Darnnell does so many things that remind me of my mom—it's wild. She speaks her mind just like my mom did. Sometimes I have to laugh and ask myself, did my brother marry our mom? Ha! I watched how my brother treated her, how he treated her friends—a gentleman, through and through.

One night we were celebrating Darnnell's birthday when they were still dating and we were at this karaoke restaurant, surrounded by all her friends. When people started leaving, my brother made sure to walk each friend to their car since it was late. Every time someone got up to go, he'd say, "I'll walk you to your car." When it was time for us to leave, it was just me, my brother, and his wife. He made sure to walk me to my car first, and then he and his wife walked to their car together. I told myself, "Yeah… my husband is going to be like that."

In my twenties and thirties, I was living life to the fullest. I was working, going to school, and being a part of a spiritual community. I enjoyed my single life! I traveled. I went to school. I wined and dined myself because I didn't need anyone else to do it for me. I bought my own diamond ring, treated myself to nice things, and genuinely loved spending time with *me*. I didn't feel like I was missing anything.

In my early twenties, I moved in with my great aunt, whom we call Aunt Shirley. She is one of the sweetest, kindest, most loving people I know. We were roomies. Aunt Shirley has been in my life since I was seven years old, or younger. Now, at ninety-two years old, she's still moving, still doing her thing. Her faith is unbelievable—no pun intended. She is one of a kind, and I love her wholeheartedly. She played a huge role in my life and I couldn't be more grateful.

My Aunt Shirley loves going to church. I used to attend regularly. Church included a set of clear and unavoidable expectations, particularly when it comes to marriage and family. Women must get married, and they should make it their life's goal. Women are seen as incomplete or somehow unfulfilled without a man.

I loved being single. I wasn't sitting around waiting for a man or society's approval. I did what worked for me. So, for anyone reading this who's single, let me say this loud and clear: Enjoy your single life. Travel. Dine out. Treat yourself. Love yourself. There's nothing wrong with being single, and you don't owe anyone an explanation for why you're not married.

For years, I thought, *Maybe marriage isn't for me.* I had solid examples of what marriage should look like and I wasn't going to accept anything less. By the time I hit my forties, I fully embraced my singledom. I wasn't bitter or longing. I loved my life, and I was good with where and who I was. I was very selective about whom I dated and who met my parents. Then—wouldn't you know it—right when I made peace with being single, my husband walked into my life.

We've been married for thirteen years, and I love it! I love my marriage. I love my husband. He's the best. He cooks! He cleans! He's been everything I didn't even know I needed. I made the decision to get married on my terms. I made the decision to stay single for a long time. I wasn't going to get married because it was expected of me or because then somehow, I would be magically complete or fulfilled. I wasn't going to get married because of society's expectations. Don't let anyone or any cultural expectation shape and define your life.

And that's the key: living life for yourself. Whether you're single, married, or somewhere in between, the point is to make choices that fit you. Not your family, not society, not anyone else. That's what I did, and I wouldn't change any part of my journey. So, if you're single, don't waste time worrying about what people think. Travel. Love yourself. Build a life that makes you happy. And if marriage is for you, great.

If it's not, that's great too. What matters is that you love you and live authentically. That's where the magic happens.

WORK AND SELF-WORTH

I did well in school. I was competitive and driven. I was always that one. You know, the one who gets the straight A's and gets called "an overachiever" because of it. Even now. People tell me I do too much. I'm doing what I want to do! Why do people label someone as an overachiever? Is it because they achieve more than what is expected? Why can't it be that the person is fully capable, aware of their potential, and determined to pursue it?

Here's the truth: I'm not an overachiever. I'm someone who understands that there's infinite potential inside me, and I want to see how far I can go. That's not extra; that's me living in alignment with who I am. I'm constantly learning, evolving, and growing—not because I have something to prove, but because I know there's more to me and I want to explore all of it.

Society tries to minimize women. Women are told to fit into neat little boxes, to behave, to tone it down, to look and act a certain way. And it's all complete bullshit. I know that I do not have to fit in and don't need society's approval. I approve of myself. That's all that matters.

WORK

My parents had good jobs. Between the two of them, they worked for three employers, stayed in the same organization for over twenty years, and then retired. That worked for them. That is not how it played out for me. I've had eleven employers—and counting!

My first job was with the Mayor's Youth Summer Program, and when I got my first paycheck, I knew—I loved having my own money. But more than that, I loved what money represented: independence, options, and yes, nice things. I love handbags. I love designer shoes and clothes. I love it all! And I don't apologize for it.

I've been working since I was sixteen without a break in employment. Every job I've had, I came in with one goal: succeed and excel. I like to be challenged. Within eighteen to twenty-four months I know the job inside and out, and it feels like the time to move on to something else. And that's exactly what I've done. But here's the thing—success as a Black woman isn't always celebrated. I've had people straight up tell me, "We don't know what to do with you" or "You'd do better in a bigger organization." Translation: I was too much for them to handle.

When I stepped into bigger organizations, I flourished, but my success wasn't always celebrated especially by folks who love the status quo. Some of my colleagues cheered me on and some saw my changes and improvements as a threat. They always thought I was coming for their job! I didn't want their job, I just wanted to do my job well. Many ambitious Black women share this experience—that tension, that inability for others to reconcile our competence with their comfort.

I advocate for myself. I self-promote. And guess what? I'm amazing at what I do. That's not arrogance; that's truth. Although my mom was my biggest cheerleader, she also sometimes admonished me as arrogant, and maybe by some definitions, I was. But what others may see as arrogance, I see as confidence.

Men do it all the time—claim their space, their ambitions, their confidence—and no one bats an eye. But for women, especially Black women, our confidence is construed as arrogance and ambition becomes aggression. I'm not apologizing for being ambitious. There is absolutely nothing wrong with being an ambitious woman. Ambition to me simply means I set objectives. I stay focused and I get things done. I see infinite potential in myself, and I'm going to explore and leverage every ounce of it. As a Black woman, I guess I'm expected to dim my light to make others comfortable. But why should I? I've worked hard to be where I am, and I'm not going to shrink myself for anyone. Not anymore.

This journey hasn't always been easy. In the workforce, I've faced challenges—people doubting me, underestimating me, and resenting me. But I've also had mentors, even the ones I didn't like, who pushed me to be better. I've learned from every experience, even the tough ones, and I'm grateful for the lessons.

Still, the challenges don't negate the truth: I'm not here to fit into anyone's box or meet anyone's expectations. I'm here to be me, fully and unapologetically.

To the women reading this—especially Black women—I want you to know this: you are enough. You don't have to prove anything to anyone. You don't have to shrink yourself or dim your light. You have infinite potential, and it's time to explore it.

Focus on yourself. Love yourself. Support other women, too. When you see another woman winning, cheer her on. Her success doesn't take away from yours. There's room for all of us. I've learned that my purpose on this planet is to be a beneficial presence, to make the world a better place. And while our missions may differ, the goal remains the same. So, find your mission. Pursue it relentlessly. And don't ever let anyone tell you that you're too much.

SPIRITUAL PRACTICE

Freedom, to me, isn't about breaking societal molds—it's about not caring what people think or say. It's about living my life fully, on my terms, and chasing the things that bring me joy unapologetically. I'm excited about who I am. I'm excited about the multi-faceted, infinite levels of me. Every day, I wake up becoming a better version of my previous self, and that's what drives me. That's what fuels me. But here's the thing—it takes work to get to this place, it doesn't just happen without effort. It takes self-reflection, introspection, and a lot of intention. For me, that's where meditation comes in.

I meditate every morning. I say affirmations and pray. Some mornings, I do visualization—visualizing the desires of my heart. Meditation isn't about sitting still or being quiet—it's about setting intentions, about waking up to who I really am. It's about quieting the noise of the world so I can really hear what's inside me.

It takes clear and focused effort to truly acknowledge and understand yourself. We are surrounded by people who are unaware of themselves and move through the world on autopilot. Humans evolve, change, and grow every single day. We become new versions of ourselves, and meditation helps me tap into my evolution. It's my space to breathe, to focus, and to connect with the real me—not the me shaped by what's in front of me, but the me I'm becoming.

Spirituality has shaped who I am and who I'm becoming. My connection with the universe, with God—whatever you want to call it—has shown me that there is enough for everyone. No shortage of success. No shortage of opportunities. No shortage of abundance. Once I understood that, I stopped competing with people. The only person I need to be better than is who I was yesterday. Spirituality isn't a part of my life—it's who I am. Although I grew up in the church and that practice gave me a great foundation, I now ask myself, *What's next? What else is out there?*

Exploring spirituality is one of my greatest joys. It's about meditation, prayer, affirmations, gratitude, and giving back. It's about circulating—circulating money, circulating good energy, circulating love. Because what you put out into the world always comes back.

Gratitude is a big part of circulating the good. Every day, I reflect on the things I'm grateful for. Sometimes it's simple:

I'm grateful to be alive. I'm grateful to have the chance to keep growing and becoming. I'm grateful to be grateful!

This journey—of exploring myself, of rejecting society's expectations, of leaning into my spirituality and my joy—it's what makes me who I am. I'm excited about life, about what's next, about everything I've yet to discover about myself. And I know this much: I'm not stopping. There's too much to explore, too much to experience, and too much of me to uncover.

So, to anyone reading this: don't let anyone tell you that you're too much, or that you're doing too much, or that you need to slow down or fit in. Be you. Explore you. Love you. And remember, you don't have to justify it to anyone. Live your life, your way, and let the rest of the world deal with it.

LETTING GO OF CONTROL

In work, in life, I was always in control. If there was a problem, I fixed it. That's what leadership teaches you—own it, manage it, control it. And that control followed me everywhere. As a meeting planner, I ran huge events—thousands of people, high-stakes logistics, contracts, and venues. If something went wrong, nobody knew because it was handled behind the scenes.

Control doesn't stay in one place. It moves into your personal life, your relationships, and how you navigate the world. At some point, you must make a choice—let go or hold on until it breaks you. Zen proverb: "Let go or be dragged." And I wasn't about to be dragged.

For years, I carried the weight of expectation, and I felt like I had to fix everything for everyone. I was the problem solver, the one who stepped up, the one who made sure things didn't fall apart. It's exhausting. Some things can't be fixed. Some things I didn't want to fix. And some things I shouldn't have even tried to fix.

I used to believe that saying "I don't know" was a weakness. In every job I had, I was told, to never say you don't know. But the opposite is true. Showing curiosity and a willingness to learn is far more powerful than pretending to know something that you do not know. Now I say, "I don't know, but let me find out." Sometimes, I don't know, and I don't care to find out. That's not my burden to carry. I have learned that not everything requires my energy.

PERFECTION IS LIMITING

Perfection? I am over it. Perfection is limiting. It keeps you stuck. It makes you feel like if something isn't flawless, then it's worthless. And that's not true. It is far from the truth.

I don't need to be perfect—I'm more than perfect. I'm growing. I'm a recovering perfectionist, and I like it that way. There are things I do not know. There are things I do not care about. And some days, I'm just not on—and I'm fine with that.

I think that shift comes with age. When you're younger, you're caught up in proving yourself. Making sure every detail is right. Doing the most. Then, you get older and realize how little of it truly matters.

Perfection doesn't validate me. Growth does. Learning does. Evolution does. I used to think that having everything in order was the key to success. But success isn't about having control over everything—it's about knowing when to let go. And I'm learning that.

UNFOLDING ME

When I look back over my life, I feel nothing but gratitude. I've come so far, and the journey keeps unfolding. I've experienced and accomplished a lot, and there's still so much left to explore. Every day, I trust myself more. I'm breaking free from society's expectations and the pressures I placed on myself.

Expectations can motivate you, but chasing perfection? That just keeps you stuck. I used to chase that idea of being the perfect person—living up to ideals that weren't even mine. Now, I'm focused on discovering who I am and becoming who I'm meant to be. Not based on what society says. Not based on what others expect. But based on who I truly am and what the Universe, God, Goddess says about me.

I'm embracing myself.

Thomas Merton said it best: "If I always remain who I am not and never become who I am meant to be, I live a life in contradiction."

I refuse to live a life in contradiction.

I love life. I love my life. I love living. And right now, I'm focused on living, discovering, and unfolding me. I've had a lot of experiences, learned a lot, and grown in ways I never expected. Life has given me opportunities to learn, to evolve, to shift. And I'm grateful for every single lesson.

I won't be defined by my past. And, your past shouldn't define you. My past is not who I am today. I'm better than I was. Much better. And what excites me the most, every single day, I get a fresh start. Some days, I catch myself wondering *What's next*? On other days I'm bored. And I ask myself, *is this just me, or is this my potential pushing me toward something bigger*? Because I know there's more.

It's discovery time for me. And yeah, there are days when I feel unmotivated or unexcited. But even in those moments, I know something greater is ahead. And that keeps me pulling forward.

Here's where I've had to check myself—I've spent so much time putting expectations on myself, telling myself, *Chanise, you gotta do this. You gotta do that. It has to happen this way.* And you know what? That kind of thinking limits me. I've realized I've been blocking myself with those expectations.

Trying to control every detail keeps me from receiving something even bigger. The universe—God, Goddess, Source Energy, whatever you want to call it—is limitless and infinite. When I tell myself that this is how it has to be, I shrink my own possibilities. I don't leave room for what's truly meant for me.

Now I'm choosing to be open. Open to what's next. Open to whatever is unfolding. Open to letting life surprise me.

Because I know, without a doubt, there are more infinite possibilities and infinite potential.

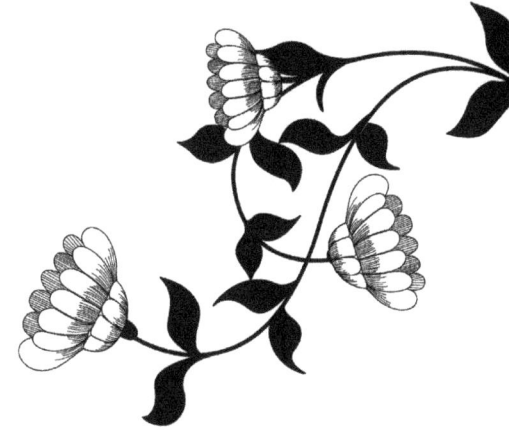

Introduction to
LASHON ORMOND

LaShon Ormond is the Chief Impact Officer at Amplify Education, where she leads the organization's impact strategy, including Innovation and Inclusion, Customer Transformation, Strategic Initiatives, Tutoring, and Customer Insights. Her role focuses on enhancing student learning outcomes and empowering educators.

Previously, LaShon was the Senior Vice President & General Manager of K-12 Humanities at Amplify. Prior to that, she served as the VP of Strategic Partnerships where she focused on strategic partnerships and project management for K-12 clients. Her leadership led to successful implementations of Amplify's initiatives in the Los Angeles Unified School District, Chicago Public Schools, and the expansion of Amplify Science within the KIPP Charter Schools.

LaShon's career demonstrates a commitment to educational excellence and large-scale initiatives. Her experience includes curriculum development, strategic partnerships, and cross-functional team leadership, which have improved Amplify's presence in major school districts.

LaShon's dedication to creating inclusive and empowering learning environments is highlighted in her work. Outside of her professional role, she is an avid reader, volunteers with organizations supporting youth and women in STEM, and owns a bookstore. She also collaborates with South African illustrator Frank Lunar on children's books. LaShon holds a BS in English and a Master of Education, and she is the mother of one daughter, Jasmyne.

In Relentless Pursuit of
SISTERHOOD

BY
LASHON ORMOND

I WAS BORN INTO THIS GIFT.

Since my arrival, I have been somebody's Sister. They greeted me upon my entrance into the world and they were great.

Great women raise great women who raise great women. It is a message inscribed on a wooden block that lives on the mantle above my fireplace. No pictures; no art; just the message that has traveled with me from North Carolina to Harlem and to the unincorporated town of Luella in the Southern Crescent of Central Georgia. Luella is too far from the city to be considered a part of Metro Atlanta, though that is what we say to the unknowing when they ask, where are you from. It is the midway point between Atlanta and Macon—because no one knows where Locust Grove is, and certainly not unincorporated Luella.

The unknowing folk's faces fall when they realize I moved here from Harlem World in NYC. How did you end up here? It's easy, I am a Southern girl. The city was good for me, for my growth, personally and professionally, but for my next stint the city was not me. It was a stop on my journey to now. And now is always evolving because that is the beauty of my life.

Beauty shows up just like the women that have walked alongside me, sometimes pushing me, sometimes pulling me along, sometimes whispering you can do it, sometimes yelling *Girl, what are you doing? Get up! Go!* But never you can't do it. The questions were always *How will I do it* and *What do I need*? Then *Why didn't you ask for help*?

Mickey says a clock is my kryptonite but asking for help is a close second. Flexibility and adaptability are both gifts and curses but I do now understand that help is not a four-letter word. Pride is, and not asking for help is evidence of a spirit of pride.

That is why I was born into this gift, to be sure that help would surround me; that it would support me and be a foundation in spite of my own efforts.

I was born into this gift and placed into my mother's arms. I took my place in the Sisterhood. I have been someone's Sister since the summer of '72. That's over fifty-two years.

I was born into this gift and surrounded by a tribe of women who would have me be:

- nothing less than all that GOD called me to be,
- nothing less than any and all that I could imagine I could be,
- nothing less than everything they prayed for me, before and after my arrival.

I was born into this gift and

- in Sisterhood they waited for me,
- in Sisterhood, they prayed for me,
- in Sisterhood, they prayed with me,
- in Sisterhood, they prayed in spite of me.

I was born into this gift and since my arrival, I have been somebody's Sister.

Like my grandmother, Agnes Marie, who was the ninth

of ten children and the youngest girl, Sisterhood waited for me; it embraced me; it made me one of its own. Our Sisterhood is a proud circle of love with outstretched arms, with treasure chests of wisdom that I sometimes accepted with joy. Sometimes I neglected this Sisterhood to my own sorrow. I was born into this gift, so aside from my parents giving me life, my grandmothers and their Sisters were the first gift givers for me and I honor them.

Before they were married, before they were wives, before they were mothers, they were Sisters and it was a bond beyond words. It was love personified and I bore witness to it early and often. Holidays, church picnics, family reunions, Saturday afternoons, Sunday mornings—on the front porch, in the kitchen or in the living room the Sisterhood lived. Hanging clothes on the lines, rejoicing at weddings, shedding tears at funerals, as ushers, grandmothers, and disciplinarians. Aunties who made the best lemon pound cake, chocolate cake with pecans, chicken salad, banana pudding and lemonade.

Sisterhood thrives and has its own gravity.

It was the collective identity they tied to their chests and their Sisterhood exceeded their time as wives. Their time as Sisters still existed when some of their children no longer walked the earth and in those burdensome moments, those moments of loss, that is when the light of the Sisterhood shone the brightest.

I was born into this gift with Agnes Marie (Ms. Marie as the community called her before she became Mother

Ormond in our church); Sallie (Aunt Sal, who experienced one hundred years of life); Thelma (mother of fifteen); Mabel (Aunt Mabel, the quilt maker); and Alice (who left us too soon) all waiting for me.

They were all waiting for *me*.

Each had their own story to tell. Each left their imprint on my life in their own unicorn way. They were the cornerstone of a village I counted on. They were the blueprint for what Sisterhood could and should be. Not perfect, often messy, sometimes nerve wracking but forever there. They protect you and they love you with unwavering faith and assurance. Sisterhood is an underestimated miracle.

I was born into this gift with Luvenia (the gardner), Julia (the educator), and Eula Mae (who had the best books and a brand-new set of encyclopedias in her home always available to me). They were my granddaddy's Sisters and my neighbors for a portion of the first decade of my life. And they became my grandmother's Sisters and especially so when granddaddy left us too soon. Each house, just a few steps from my grandma's. Grandma's and Aunt Veenie's houses, only separated by the garden they planted and tended together. Aunt Veenie's yard was adorned with vibrant hydrangea bushes. Aunt Veenie's house and Aunt Eula Mae's house were separated by one street, too wide for me to jump over but narrow enough for me to cross on my own! Aunt Julia was just a bike ride or a truck ride away. I rode with granddaddy in a bumpy red Chevy, and we went to see Uncle Jasper, his big brother.

I was born into this gift.

My mom had three Sisters: Elma Grey who gave birth to my oldest cousin and best babysitter in the world. Thelma was wise and instructive, whose second born was more like a little brother. Sandra Gail was the baby of them all, who offered me a part in her wedding, a seat in her salon, and access to her closet. A college friend compared us to the tribes of Amazon women—wonderwomen, he'd said. We were like mythical beings. He was right. We are a tribe, and I savored the comparison. He saw love, protection, strength and a community within me.

I was born into this gift and since my arrival, I have been somebody's Sister.

My mom's Sisters cared for me while my mom worked because that's what Sisters do. They combed my hair, got me dressed for school, reminded me that I was a little girl, and made me come inside and take baths when I'd rather be outside playing. When my Aunt Gail married and moved to Durham, it meant summer vacations in the city and that was a new experience for me and for my Sister. It expanded our understanding of the world. And it was a welcome break for my mom.

I was born into this gift, as if God knew what he'd have me do because the Sisterhood was present with my Dad's family too.

Ida Mae, my Dad's mama, who according to my favorite Olds' girl cousin, Christa, told her and her brothers that I was special and that I was different—unlike my

Mom's mom, where I declared myself to be her favorite (because it was true). And her Sisters: Mable Lee, Mittie, Bea, Lucinda, Sandy, Ellen, Bessie. And my Granddaddy's Sisters: Bruce, Alma.

Because of Grandma Ida and the Wilkes/Olds tribe, I traveled to Washington, DC, Delaware, New York, New Jersey, and Pennsylvania. Aunt Mittie's house was our own underground railroad stop. It was where members of our family participating in The Great Migration paused, gathered themselves and planned their futures after escaping the Jim Crow South. The South was filled with hate but not enough hate to disrupt the love expressed through the gift I was born into. Our Sisterhood was stronger than their hate.

I was born into this gift with Kimberly Denise, my own big Sister, protector, fashion coordinator, hair stylist, and encourager, and my ultimate cheerleader. In school and when family members couldn't remember my name, her name became my name too (like John Jacob Jingleheimer Schmidt). That's Kim's little Sister, they'd say. And my teachers, who once taught her, called me Kim, too. Some of those days I did not embrace the Sisterhood gift.

I was born into this gift and since my arrival, I have been somebody's Sister.

My earliest days were filled with a network of expectation and a promise of joy and community. Their stories weren't made-for-TV movies or even the big screen. Theirs were stories of resilience and perseverance, determination and abundant happiness. Joy is emphasized because Black

Woman Joy is revolutionary and unexpected. But it is. It does exist. It is real. And it is good.

I was born into this gift and was allowed to sit at the feet of the Sisterhood and watch them shell peas, mix corn meal, and squeeze lemons. I watched them peel sweet potatoes, chop collards, and add a dash of vanilla extract to the cake batter and a pinch of sugar to the corn bread.

I was born into this gift, and it was a tapestry of saying and not saying, knowing and nodding, woven by hand and by heart like Aunt Mabel's handmade quilts. It was the thread that connected their hearts when their hands were not enough. The gift was warm; it was comforting and sometimes it was heavy, like when Aunt Alice didn't recover from the accident from the hurricane or when granddaddy took his last breath. Their bond was beyond their shared DNA.

I was born into this gift, and it was the compass that guided my friendships. It was how I wanted to live my life, building communities of friendship, support and love.

There's a photograph that I keep on my phone. It is of my grandmother and her Sisters, showing them standing shoulder to shoulder—a black and white snapshot of Sisterhood and solidarity. I often look at it, searching for clues about my legacy, about how these women, steadfast and determined, shaped the soul of a girl like me. Their impact is whispered in the echoes of my life, guiding me quietly yet persistently, urging me towards nurturing bonds of my own.

I was born into this gift and my grandmothers and their Sisters, my mom and her Sisters and my Dad's Sisters set the stage for a legacy of fierce loyalty and support; and unyielding love, love without regard; love without demands; just love.

I was born into this gift and since my arrival, I was somebody's Sister, enveloped in lessons of unity and strength. Through a symphony of memories, I was shaped by the melody of their stories. It was a masterclass in defying the preconceived notions of small-southern-town Black girl existence and the expansion of the opportunities of those in their charge—and I was in their charge.

I was born into this gift, and it called me to explore and embrace an unknown world, one in which the safety and sanctity of my earliest years and most beautiful memories did not know. Though I left, I knew it wouldn't leave me, and I knew that there was a road back there, with warmth and words waiting to welcome me home.

I was born into this gift, and it tested me from time to time. Like when the summer camp director said derogatory things to the little girls in my camp group, questioning what they could and could not have in their homes, threatening to hurt and harm members of my Sisterhood. I heard the collective voice of my gift asking *Are you your Sister's keeper?* Of course I am; of course I know what to do. I spoke up and honored the Sisterhood, I did not let the moment pass without comment and correction.

I was born into this gift, but I didn't always model the

gift. I didn't always keep the secret or sacrifice for another. Sometimes I betrayed the gift. Sometimes I betrayed The Sisterhood. I was growing and learning.

I was born into this gift, and it provided me with an education in empathy and understanding, demonstrating the essence of mutual respect and open-hearted listening.

Through the laughter, tears, and sheer messiness of life, they showed me that harboring such bonds demands patience and compromise; yet the rewards far surpass any investment. They taught me that the strength of Sisterhood resides as much in the silences as it does in words, as much in shared hardships as in joyous celebrations.

In those moments where they enveloped me with their love and wisdom, I learned a vital truth: to be somebody's Sister is both a privilege and a responsibility. The legacy they constructed is one where love is a verb, an active pursuit shaped by deeds, not just intentions. They taught me that to be a Sister is to be eternal, an ever-present heartbeat within the family, a constant reminder of the kindness the world so desperately needs.

I was born into this gift, and it was greater than the girl code. The girl code was important, but the gift of Sisterhood was even more so. It demanded vision and presence and forgiveness and possibility in the face of frustration. It meant swallowing *I told you so* in favor of hugs, and wiping away tears because I am my Sister's keeper.

I was born into this gift, a legacy that was shared not only physically but spiritually and emotionally; a collection of dreams deferred and hopes realized; a history of manifested moments, minutes and memories. It is anchored in shared yesterdays and powered by imagined tomorrows. The gift carries with it a sacred and unspoken promise that better was closer than the comfort of the beforeness of yesterday.

I was born into this gift, and it said *I will help you if you let me, but I cannot make you let go of what is attempting to lessen you. I cannot lead you beyond the longing of last night, last week, last month, last year if you do not let me.*

I was born into this gift, and I took it for granted. I had never not known the gathering of women. I had never not known the love of Sisters. As I traversed through young adulthood, the gift was ever present. It taught me to be selective in my choosing but never to be exclusionary. Everyone deserved community and mine was a space where they could fill and be filled.

As the years progressed, I appreciated the subtle, intricate dance of Sisterhood as demonstrated by my grandmother and her Sisters. It was a choreography of empathy and humor, a balancing act of giving space and holding close. In a world where change is the only constant, their enduring connection stood as a testament to the resilience of the human spirit. I realized I was watching a masterclass on life and understanding, delivered with each look exchanged between them. The gift I was born into set the stage for a legacy of fierce loyalty and unyielding love, one I aspired to emulate and pass on.

I was born into this gift and since my arrival, I have been somebody's Sister.

The universe blessed me with a grandmother and a mother whose strength and compassion were mirrored in their own Sisters. They created a safety net woven tightly with devotion, ensuring that someone was always there to watch over me. They were the eternal guardians of my peace, the architects of my safe haven. They still are.

My mother and her Sisters fashioned a microcosm of love and accountability, each one's role as protectress imprinted upon me at an early age. I knew, no matter where the winds of life blew me, their gaze rested on me, like sentinels watching the boundaries of a kingdom. Their unconditional support allowed me to flourish, knowing that I was never alone.

I was born into this gift and since my arrival, I have been somebody's Sister. Yet, as my journey unfolded, I discovered that Sisterhood stretched beyond familial confines into the realms of friendship—those vibrant connections born from shared experiences and mutual trust. College became the crucible within which my Sisterhood with friends was forged, an unexpected but life-affirming kinship.

The evolution from friends to Sisters was an organic, albeit complex process marked by late-night study sessions that transformed into philosophical debates about our lives, our futures, and the imprint we wished to leave upon the world. My college friends became my chosen Sisters, and together we created a village of strength and resilience. Our backgrounds varied, our individual stories unique, yet our desire for community bound us tightly together. Even this was a reflection of the gift I was born into.

Our journey to Sisterhood was built on small acts of kindness—shared care packages during exams, a shoulder to lean on during heartbreaks, cheers of encouragement during moments of doubt. They became my sounding board and my biggest champions, sharing in both my failures and triumphs as though they were their own.

This mosaic of Sisterhood expanded as we ventured into the wider world. We became village keepers, staunch advocates for each other's dreams, and defenders against humanity's inexorable challenges. Through fostering such bonds, I realized that life often places these people in our paths to remind us of what truly matters—the connections we build and the hearts we uplift.

In choosing each other, we became more than friends; we became Sisters. Ours was a pact to nurture and grow together, to laugh and learn, to survive and thrive. This journey illuminated the boundless nature of Sisterhood—that it is not confined by biology or geography but spirited by love and mutual respect.

I have spent my life in relentless pursuit of Sisterhood, cherishing each thread of the vast and colored tapestry that defines my journey. It is a legacy passed on by generations of women who lived before me and one that I pass to those who come after. Through every chapter, every story, I rediscovered the truth at the heart of Sisterhood: It is an eternal symphony, a continuous gift, and the greatest of blessings.

I was born into this gift and since my arrival, I have been somebody's Sister.

As my understanding of Sisterhood deepened, I found another dimension within the walls of my faith tradition and church family. It was here that I became Sister LaShon—a title not just signifying respect but encapsulating a spiritual bond that transcended the ordinary rhythms of life. In our congregation, Sisterhood was spoken in the language of grace and rooted in shared beliefs.

Each Sunday, as the choir's harmonies filled the sanctuary, I sat surrounded by women who embodied compassion and resilience. Our faith knitted us together, creating a spiritual mosaic in which each of our lives was a vital, irreplaceable piece. Here, I learned that Sisterhood in faith was not bound merely by communal worship but extended into everyday acts of kindness—a meal cooked for a grieving family, prayers whispered for the sick, laughter shared over brunch after service.

Becoming Sister LaShon meant stepping into roles as both a learner and a teacher, participating in Bible studies, leading youth groups, and engaging in outreach programs. As I gathered with these women under the loving guidance of our faith, there was a profound sense of belonging and encouragement to explore my spirituality more deeply. We were each other's confidantes and counsel, finding strength in collective prayers, feeling God's presence in each other's lives.

This Sisterhood offered more than solace; it instilled purpose. It encouraged me to be the best version of myself, urging me to look beyond the walls of the physical church and take my faith into the wider community. As Sister LaShon, I was not merely a member of a congregation—I was a part of a unifying force, a testament to the transformative power of faith and community.

I was born into this gift and since my arrival, I have been somebody's Sister.

As life's mosaic rearranged its pieces, fate bestowed upon me the role of a big Sister—a serendipitous twist that came later in my path when my father remarried and brought a new little Sister into our family fold. This new chapter in life redefined my understanding of what it meant to be a Sister. Just as my big Sister shielded and guided me, I embraced my duty towards this sweet, yet sometimes bewildering, little girl now under my wing. Our relationship began as an uncharted territory, her eyes reflecting both curiosity and affection as she navigated this new sibling dynamic.

As her big Sister, I found joy in teaching her the lessons learned from the women in our lineage, of courage and empathy, of laughter's power to heal. My role was dual, both a protector and a friend—much like my own Sister had once been for me.

Watching her grow into her own individuality, full of dreams and aspirations, filled me with pride and a renewed sense of purpose. I realized that the greatest gift of being somebody's Sister was the opportunity to influence a life by simply being present. My promise to her was unwavering support and love, to be her anchor and her cheering squad in equal measure.

My journey as a big Sister became a reflection of the continuum of Sisterhood—a never-ending loop of guidance and grace, reminding me that I continue to hold pieces of those who came before me and those yet to come in my heart.

I was born into this gift and since my arrival, I have been somebody's Sister.

Sometimes, I am saddened because I didn't give my daughter that precious gift of sisterhood in the traditional familial structure, but I try to help her identify opportunities that enable her to build that which she didn't get from me. I also encourage her to see the possibility in her relationships with her father's daughters. They are her Sisters too. And I try to help her see it in my relationships with my best friends and her godmother.

My Sister and I celebrate my grandmother and her Sisters in our retelling of their stories and by honoring their sacrifices. We do that because we understand the gift that we were born into and we want that for our daughters and our nieces.

I was born into this gift and since my arrival, I have been somebody's Sister.

As my life intersected with new environments, I discovered that Sisterhood was not confined to friends, family or faith. At work emerged another variant—colleagues turned work besties turned Sisters, a chosen family forged in the shared trenches of professional pursuits.

Navigating the world of work was unpredictable, filled with challenges and aspirations alike, and my work besties became a steadfast anchor through every storm. Together, we navigated office politics, tackled complex projects, celebrated milestones, and supported each other through personal triumphs and trials. The bonds of Sisterhood were sewn with humor over lunch and on trips across the country, whispered encouragement before daunting meetings, and empathy in moments of doubt.

These women were more than coworkers; they were a lifeline—a reminder that we thrive not in isolation but in unity. They were my compass, helping me navigate the intricacies of a career journey while reminding me of the importance of balance and authenticity. With them, I was both a sounding board and a trusted ally, their sage advice often lighting my path forward.

Through our professional alliance, we chose to cover each other, offering a protective weave against the unpredictable winds of life's demands. The essence of our work Sisterhood was rooted in mutual respect, laughter, and the shared understanding that the aspiration for success was greater together.

Choosing them and being chosen in return created a tapestry of support—resilient threads that carried me through the ebbs and flows of professional life. In these alliances, I found yet another testament to the transformative power of Sisterhood—a power that extended beyond bloodlines and into every facet of existence, highlighting the beauty in choosing and being chosen.

I was born into this gift and since my arrival, I have been somebody's Sister.

Over the years, I embraced this identity wholly, understanding that the blessings of Sisterhood are interwoven with an unyielding purpose—to make a difference, to uplift and inspire others, particularly women and girls.

From the time I was a teenager serving as a volunteer at a summer camp for younger girls, my heart understood the importance of stewardship, the necessity of being my Sister's keeper. I saw in their eyes the same yearnings and aspirations that once filled my own youth. It was here that I realized protecting and empowering women and girls was not merely an act of guidance but a calling for my life.

Throughout my journey, one core truth stood unwavering: Sisterhood is not solely about nurturing those you know; it is about extending a hand to every woman you encounter. It is about building bridges rather than drawing boundaries—it is about inciting courage where there is fear and encouraging dreams to take flight.

In every interaction, I transform the mundane to meaningful, driven by an intrinsic desire to see women thrive and realize their fullest potential. Whether through mentorship, advocacy, or simply listening, my mission echoes the call of those trailblazing women from whom I draw inspiration—a call to be an everlasting force for good.

By pushing each woman toward her dreams, offering encouragement, and providing the occasional nudge toward a brighter future, I fulfill a legacy passed down through countless generations of Sisters. For I am not just born into this gift of Sisterhood; I am tasked with carrying it forward—with grace, strength, and above all, love.

In these pursuits, I remain a steadfast believer that the essence of Sisterhood lies not just in the ties that bind but in the hearts we touch, in the dreams we ignite, and in the courage we inspire. Through every act of Sisterhood, we create a more significant ripple in the oceans of life, leaving an indelible legacy of kindness for those who come after us.

I was born into this gift and since my arrival, I have been somebody's Sister.

EPILOGUE

WE SAT ON A ZOOM CALL and each face in the little windows looked excited and nervous. Authors often enter the journey of publication with trepidation, concern, and hopefulness. I have done many of these by now, but this kick-off call had a new element. I was the only white face on the screen. Although it is common for me to be the only female on a business Zoom call, rarely, if ever, am I the only white person. Often there are none, or only one or two Black or brown faces on the calls I attend for my day job. My work with Hunter Street Press is far more consistently diverse, but this was new.

These brave Black female authors asked how I approached editing. They discussed their concern about their words being diminished or *white-washed*, their chapters moved across my desk. This was an element that I had never considered (an unrealized privilege). This was even after working with the authoritative Dominique Luster on previous projects and thought I understood the power of authorship, archival, and editing.

I fumbled through an explanation of my process, how I find their voice and only level up the work in literary quality and norms. Thankfully, Ronicka assured these beautiful women that their stories and words would be honored, which she knew from working with me previously. The group largely seemed to accept my inclusion and role. A few folks said they were placing their trust in Ronicka and were still unsure.

I am endlessly thankful they shared their words with me

and entrusted me with the important work of line editing (literary up-leveling). I stayed true to their voice and the message they wanted to share. I do this with all authors I work with, but this group's concern stayed front of mind while I worked on the principal effort. I am grateful to have an opportunity to participate and contribute to this project. It is essential work, it is crucial that Black and brown peoples are given the authority to share their lived experiences.

The Unicorn Effect, related to the 10 Times Rule, has driven these women to perform and live beyond typical expectations. The pressure to be always phenomenal is unfair, unrealistic, and fundamentally wrong. It is imperative that all of us drive and demand change. The expectations, realities, and the collective lived experiences of Black women must evolve beyond where we stand as a Western society today.

These stories have several common themes. Firstly, these women accepted the challenges they faced and pushed beyond regardless. There is not a single author in this work that played the victim. They understood their position and knew they must outperform their counterparts. They nearly worked themselves to death and all of them poured from empty cups at some point. They learned the importance of holding enough space for themselves and how to ask for help. Each of these women have colorful and robust family lives, and the importance of family is front-and-center. Their foundation is family and faith, and they are driven to help their community. They are not only focused on their lives, but the lives of Black, brown, and minority communities. They will not rest until the next generation feels the positive results of their work.

LaShon's poetry of Sisterhood applies to these authors. This Sisterhood is established and cherished. This Sisterhood carries the blood and the power of the prior generations of women and will continue to those who come after. LaShon reminds us "Sisterhood is not solely about nurturing those you know; it is about extending a hand to every woman you encounter. It is about building bridges rather than drawing boundaries—it is about inciting courage where there is fear and encouraging dreams to take flight."

I am so honored (yes, I know I keep using this word, but the thesaurus does not have any other word that seems as appropriate) to have played a tiny role in letting these respected and formidable women share their stories. Dominique's words are so powerful and applicable: "History tends to favor the ones who write it down." It is imperative we share these women's stories and their lived experiences. And now, more than ever, we must ensure that all people, particularly Black, brown, and minorities, are seen, and treated, as equal humans.

APPENDIX

VISUALIZING THE UNICORN EFFECT

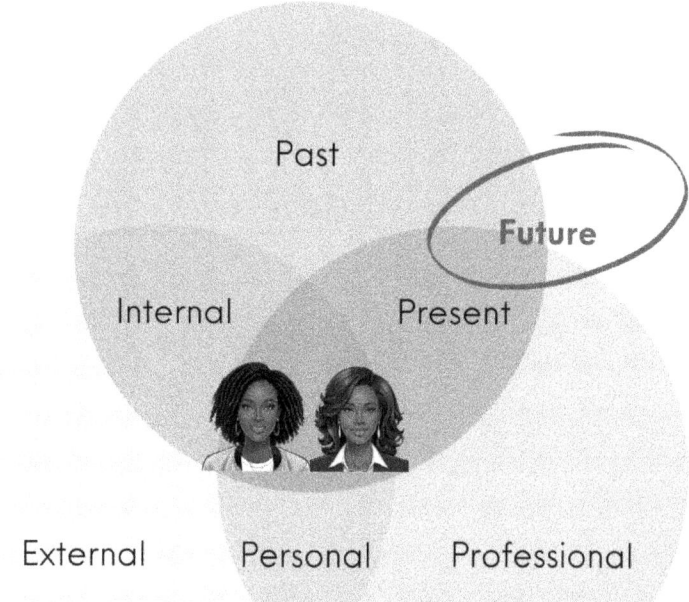

AUTOETHNOGRAPHY EXPLAINED

Autobiography

self-written account of a person's life

Ethnography

involves the in-depth study of people, cultures, and social interactions within their natural environments

Autoethnography

It allows us to examine our lived experiences through a broader cultural and societal lens, connecting the personal to the systemic.

UNPACKING THE UNICORN EFFECT

Use this template to reflect on and identify how you've personally experienced the Unicorn Effect in your life and leadership.

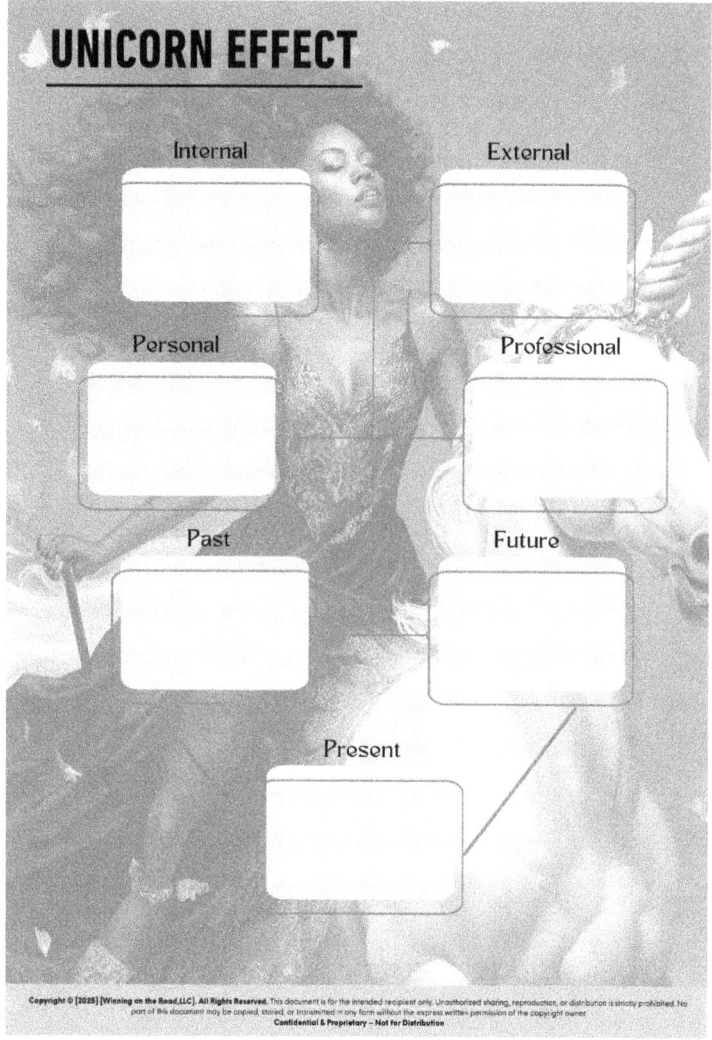

ACKNOWLEDGEMENTS

PRAISES TO THE MOST HIGH GOD, who orchestrates every detail of our lives with divine precision. It was only through His grace and perfect timing that this dynamic group of brilliant, bold, and beautiful women came together to bring *In Relentless Pursuit of Me* to life.

To each contributing author—thank you. Your willingness to join me on this journey, especially as I stepped into the world of publishing for the first time, means more than words can express. Your stories are powerful, and your vulnerability is a gift to every reader who will be transformed by your truth.

This book was birthed from my doctoral dissertation, where I had the sacred privilege of interviewing extraordinary Black women leaders. As they shared their stories, it became clear—each woman was navigating something powerful, something that didn't yet have a name, but was deeply felt and undeniably real. And I knew: how we define the problem shapes the solutions we pursue. So, I gave it a name—*The Unicorn Effect*. I'm forever grateful to the women who trusted me with their stories and laid the foundation for this work.

To Hope Mueller of Hunter Street Press—thank you for being not only a skilled publisher and managing editor, but also a friend. Your guidance, patience, and reverence for each woman's story have been a blessing.

To our incredible book designer, Tara, and our thoughtful and meticulous copy editor, Dick Mueller—thank you both for lending your gifts so generously to this project.

Your work brought this vision to life in ways that exceeded expectations.

To everyone who has supported this project—whether cheering us on from afar, sharing online, or encouraging me in real life—your love is deeply felt and appreciated.

To my sister, Aaron—thank you for always being a sounding board, a partner in planning, and a steady source of unconditional love.

And to my mom, Marichell—affectionately known as Ma, she's my rider, my biggest cheerleader, and the greatest granny nanny of all time—thank you for being everything I never have to ask for.

And my husband, Wilbert—thank you for being my peace, my strength, and my constant. Your love makes it possible for me to chase my dreams without hesitation. To our two amazing children, Carley and Wilbert Jr.—watching you grow and support this journey with such grace fills my heart with pride and joy.

This book is for every woman who is in relentless pursuit of herself. May you see yourself reflected in these pages and know that you, too, are magic.

And we know that all things work together for good to them that love God, to them who are the called according to his purpose (Romans 8:28 KJV).

DISCUSSION GUIDE QUESTIONS

IN RELENTLESS PURSUIT OF BEING MY VOICE

1. The chapter illustrates how the Unicorn Effect influences which opportunities Black women accept, often at their own expense. How have you witnessed or experienced this pressure to say *yes* to opportunities that don't fully align with your true desires?

2. The author describes moments when she "turned down the volume on her internal wisdom." Reflect on a time when you ignored your inner voice to meet external expectations. What were the consequences?

3. The chapter ends with an ongoing commitment to "showing up for myself." What strategies have you found effective in prioritizing your authentic self?

IN RELENTLESS PURSUIT OF ENOUGHNESS

1. What does "enough" truly mean to you, and how has that definition changed over time?

2. How does the theme of "In Relentless Pursuit of Enoughness" resonate with your own experiences? Have there been moments in your life where you felt caught in the cycle of proving, striving, or questioning your sense of enough?

3. In what ways has the pressure to constantly prove your worth shaped your decisions, and how might your life look if you embraced the idea that you are already enough?

IN RELENTLESS PURSUIT OF AUTONOMY

1. What does autonomy look like for you? Are you striving to achieve an autonomous life?

2. Think about some of the core beliefs you developed in childhood. How have they impacted you in adulthood?

3. Are there times when you (irrationally) didn't feel good enough despite your many achievements? Pinpoint the negative thoughts that are fueling your feelings of unworthiness.

4. Describe a time when you sacrificed your own happiness/freedom to maintain a difficult job or relationship. Why did you settle?

5. What dream would you pursue if you weren't afraid to fail? Reflect on the obstacles preventing you from making your dream a reality.

IN RELENTLESS PURSUIT OF LEGACY

1. The author speaks to the power of curating history and legacy, an understanding that history-making is an active process. How are you actively building your legacy? What decisions, values, or work in your life are shaping the legacy you will leave behind?

2. With all the expectations placed on women, how might societal norms and expectations—good or bad—impact our willingness to ask for help? When have you stayed silent out of shame or fear, and what did it cost you?

3. Have you experienced a personal or professional redirection driven by circumstance? Were you able to recognize it as a painful detour that might be part of a larger calling?

4. Where in your life are you "smiling and waving" while struggling inside? What would it look like to show up more authentically, and what would you need to do that?

IN RELENTLESS PURSUIT OF PEACE

1. The author describes feeling frozen while standing over her mother's body—a moment of deep shock and trauma. Have you ever experienced a time when your body or emotions shut down in response to grief or overwhelming pain? How did you eventually find peace in that moment or in the healing that followed?

2. The author reflects on how certain relationships and experiences challenged her sense of identity and self-worth. Can you recall a time when someone's actions—or your own—forced you to re-examine how you saw yourself? How did you find peace within yourself through that process of self-reflection?

3. The author shares the saying, "People are in your life for a reason or a season," as she looked back on a painful friendship that helped her grow. Have you experienced a relationship that felt hurtful at the time but taught you something meaningful in hindsight? How did finding peace with that relationship shape your personal growth?

4. Considering what you've learned about the "unicorn effect," where being seen as unique, strong, or exceptional can sometimes lead to invisibility when struggling, how have you developed coping habits that help you find peace amidst life's pressures? What practices or habits have helped you navigate challenges and maintain inner calm?

IN RELENTLESS PURSUIT OF PURPOSE

1. On your way to fulfilling your purpose, how do you show up boldly in spaces and places when it is not always comfortable?

2. What approaches have you taken to uncover your gifts, talents, and ultimate purpose?

3. Why is it essential to have trusted advisors, mentors, and/or personal and professional coaches?

4. How much consideration do you give to connecting with your circle of advisors? Does your circle include peers, contemporaries, individuals of different genders, races, and those outside your field or from diverse backgrounds?

5. How have your advisors enriched your journey?

6. Discuss how your mentor and coaching circle evolved?

IN RELENTLESS PURSUIT OF MY INFINITE POTENTIAL

1. What parts of yourself are you still discovering, and how are you making space for that growth?

2. Are you living by your own truth, or by expectations others have placed on you?

3. Where in your life do you feel the need to release control to allow something greater to unfold?

4. How have your past experiences shaped you, and in what ways do you want to stop letting them define you?

5. What does living fully look like for you in this season of your life?

IN RELENTLESS PURSUIT OF SISTERHOOD

1. How does the concept of "Black Woman Joy" serve as a revolutionary act according to the essay? Discuss the significance of joy in challenging societal expectations and norms.

2. The essay mentions that the bond of Sisterhood is beyond shared DNA. What elements are highlighted as essential in forming and sustaining these bonds? Reflect on personal experiences where bonds were formed beyond biological ties.

3. What lessons about empathy and understanding does the narrator gain from being part of this Sisterhood?

How can these lessons be applied in fostering relationships in diverse or multicultural settings?

4. How is the strength of Sisterhood portrayed in silence and shared hardships, as well as in joyous celebrations? Can you think of situations where solidarity is expressed non-verbally or through shared experiences?

5. The transformation from friendship to Sisterhood in a college setting is mentioned as an organic yet complex process. What factors contribute to this evolution, and how does college life facilitate such deep connections?

JOURNALING ACTIVITY:

Reflect on a community or group that has significantly shaped your values or identity. Consider areas such as empathy, shared experiences, or the sense of belonging. In your journal, write about how this group influenced you and how you, in turn, contributed to the community. Additionally, explore how these experiences have informed your understanding of Sisterhood or camaraderie.

DISCUSSION GUIDE QUESTIONS | 201

www.ingramcontent.com/pod-product-compliance
Lightning Source LLC
Chambersburg PA
CBHW051615010526
44107CB00037B/1431/J